ROY LEVY
WITH GAIL MEJIA

GAIL's
ARTISAN BAKERY

COOKBOOK

EBURY
PRESS

CONTENTS

FOREWORD BY GAIL MEJIA

I can't bake to save my life! Not bread, not cake, not anything. I never could, and I doubt I ever will. Yet my ventures over the last twenty years in London revolved around bread and baking. At the outset buying, selling and distributing bread and other baked products, and later on opening Baker & Spice and then GAIL's, each with baking at their heart. A life of baking in my head, and vicariously through the wonderfully talented people who worked with me and were able to interpret and bring to life some seriously mad notions. Baking, for me, has always been an intellectual exercise.

I love food but especially bread. Good simple food, with minimum fuss and even less ingredients, is happiness. I determined a long time ago that my last meal would be a slice of sourdough with French sweet butter and slices of ripe tomato sprinkled with sea salt.

I was already baking and distributing on a fair scale for the wholesale market in London when in 1995 an opportunity presented itself in the form of an old historical bakery and shop on Walton Street in London. The shop was tiny, a shoebox, but it had a substantial kitchen in the back with a bakery downstairs. Being rather impulsive I wanted to open a shop that would sell only what was made on the premises. That bakery downstairs was key to this idea, because down a rickety and wholly illegal wooden flight of stairs lay two monster ovens, possibly 150 years old, holding up the building above our heads. They were massive old flat-stone ovens and they worked.

It was scary and exciting and we set about trying to make bread as it was done 100 years earlier. It was at this precise point, reading bread recipes in books from around the world, that I discovered baking in my head. I could taste the bread in my mind as I was reading the recipes, and when we made some of them I knew with complete certainty what I wanted them to taste like.

Industrial food manufacturing I reasoned, is all about pretend food, making a mockery of what we are all forced to do, eat every day. I wanted to do it right and do it as well as we can. Good bread with a significant flavour profile takes time. Time is money. If you take time out of the equation you end up in Chorleywood, and the product most people consume in the UK. I call it 'the product' because bread it isn't.

I was always interested in politics and dealing with food; buying for the business, making food and selling to the public brought with it a heightened sense of responsibility. People are actually eating what we cooked and baked; this had better be excellent in every sense. I cannot pretend to have arrived fully formed. I developed my theories as I went along. I am old enough to remember what good produce used to taste like before food became a global disaster, I knew about seasonality and geography, and got interested in sustainable and organic agriculture.

We fired up the flame-throwing monsters in the basement of what became Baker & Spice, and through trial and error and not following the rules because we didn't know them, out popped the most amazing bread. Mastering the art of baking with a sole oven is a process. You must befriend the beast and learn to recognize the hot spots and cooler climes in the chamber. We had our fair share of burnt offerings, under-bakes and all manner of disasters. We buried the failures and thought and baked our way into some absolute crackers, iconic examples that are still there, on the shelves of every GAIL's shop to this day, nearly 20 years later.

I was bloody lucky with the people I worked with; Roy Levy being the ultimate soul mate. We elected to work mainly with sourdoughs and if you think that long slow fermentations are a leisurely affair you could not be more wrong. Sourdoughs, like people, are alive, temperamental and need constant care and supervision. My sourdoughs travelled the world and they are still going strong in GAIL's bakery today, over 18 years later. This is the magic of the continuum, they were the heart and soul of the bread we made, and they still are.

Given the right conditions and training most people will actively choose to do well. Somehow, unspoken, we collectively decided that whatever we made we should always strive to create the best in class.

Several years had passed when one day I get a phone call from a stranger. Ran Avidan wanted to chat about an idea involving bread. Ran and his friend Tom Molnar had their own bread obsessions. They thought that London was poorly served with real quality bread and wanted to establish neighbourhood café-bakeries. I loved the idea and we decided to work together to make this happen.

GAIL's was born in Hampstead in June 2005. And she was beautiful. I designed a shop with a small bakery and kitchen in the back. We were bakers and we were going to bake in that shop daily. The window display, dominated by beautiful bread and pastries, left no doubts as to what we were about. Care was lavished on systems that ensured we never compromised the quality and integrity of what we made. I had great misgivings about putting my name above the door knowing full well that I would not be there forever but the quality continues under Roy's sure hand and the dedication of a fantastic team of bakers who worked with me for so many years.

There is a strong thread linking my first shop and my last. In retrospect I realise that I developed my own food language. Notwithstanding the size of the business, bread is made the same way as when this journey began in Walton Street.

Despite the fact that until fairly recently most Londoners had no easy access to real bread, they recognised it when they saw it. I believe we are programmed with the love of bread in our DNA.

This book is about much more than bread. I hope, that the abiding idea everyone takes away from reading this book is how not to follow recipes. The thread that runs through it is that nobody will take care of our wellbeing more seriously than us.

Working through these recipes will involve trials and errors and practicing on your friends and family will undoubtedly make you the most popular person on the block. This book reflects a labour of love over many years; I hope you enjoy the journey as much as I have.

Gail Mejia
Co-founder

INTRODUCTION

In a world of email signatures and funny job titles, I'm happy to say I bake for a living.

I wasn't always a baker – I wasn't even trained as one – but baking found me and I'm grateful to have discovered something I love doing. Waking up early, going to say hello to my doughs and sourdough starters, firing up the ovens before other people's days have even begun – this is my idea of heaven. When you take something beautiful and delicious out of the oven at 6 a.m., you know that the rest of your day can't possibly go wrong.

But then I set to work on this book – and I realised that it was the one thing I had no recipe for. Writing this book has turned out to be one of the most difficult things I've ever done, even though baking and writing a cookbook are more similar than I'd realised. You write a book with an audience in mind, just like you bake a cake – because you want someone to eat it. In both cases, you're putting a piece of yourself out there, and hoping that someone, somewhere, will appreciate it. Becoming a good baker is having the confidence to bring yourself to the bowl and the table. Some people will tell you that the most important ingredient is time, while I think that the most precious one is you.

I'm lucky to have had the chance to write this book, not least because the writing process has helped me become a better baker. It has made me question everything we do at GAIL's – Why this? Is this worth including? Is this necessary? It has meant taking knowledge that is born of years of trial and error, habit and experience – things that a baker knows instinctively and almost on an unconscious level – and figuring out how to transmit that knowledge to another person. It's like telling a story. When I understood that, things became slightly easier. It was a breakthrough.

There's still a lot of silly, intimidating language that surrounds baking, so the sooner you can forget it, the better. Some people will try to tell you that baking is a science. Ignore them. Humans have been baking for thousands of years, long before modern science existed. If people could bake sourdough loaves 2,000 years ago then, honestly, you'll manage just fine in your twenty-first-century kitchen with all the mod cons. Others say it's an art: it isn't, and it isn't magic or alchemy either.

Baking is a simple craft and I honestly believe that learning to bake involves rediscovering how to use a part of our body and brain – a reflex that we've neglected and forgotten about, but that we all have. It's our human need to create: to take two things, put them together and see if we can make something totally new out of them. The world we live in doesn't always allow us many ways to express ourselves, but baking is a humble but very beautiful way to do so. Baking will help you discover your intuition and those latent muscles. It's all there; you only need to bring it back to life. When you knead and work the dough, you'll be performing an action that connects you to thousands of years of tradition.

GAIL's is an artisan bakery. It's all about craftsmanship and the human element. The recipes I've gathered here are not just scaled-back versions of what I bake for our customers at GAIL's every day. Instead I completely rethought and re-imagined them for the home baker and kitchen. I put them through a rigorous and uncompromising process of testing to make them suitable for that. I might be an expert in making a baker's dozen of loaves, but when I went to bake just one it was a total failure. I had to retrain myself and go right back to basics. Then, once we'd got our recipes right, we insisted on testing them all with the most commonplace equipment we could get hold of. It turns out there's nothing like a mediocre oven and a broken spatula to really check that a recipe really

works. We tried and tweaked and tested the recipes endlessly on friends, family and customers who aren't bakers, creating our own little community of bread heads until we were happy. Exhausted, sure, but happy.

This book isn't about an abstract idea of creating the perfect cake or loaf, it's about unleashing your creativity and discovering the pleasure that I've found in baking. You don't necessarily need an audience to applaud perfection, just hungry friends and family. The story begins with a few common ingredients and ends with a huge sense of satisfaction. As your confidence increases, you can add your own elements to the story. Allow yourself to be open to surprise and 'happy accidents'. The perfect loaf won't appear to be the most beautiful one though. Sometimes the most misshapen, weird looking croissant on the tray is the tastiest one, I say.

Roy Levy

THE GAIL'S STORY

In 2005, we set out with a dream to make beautiful bread more accessible. It seemed crazy to us that there were so few quality neighbourhood bakeries in the UK, and we wanted to do our bit to change that. Things are much better now, and it's a little easier to get a decent loaf of bread, but there's still a long way to go. This book grew out of the same dream that inspired us right at the start: now anyone – no matter where they live – can bring a bit of GAIL's into their own home.

GAIL's was born in Hampstead in June 2005. We designed a corner shop with a small bakery and kitchen in the back – small, but perfectly formed. The window display, dominated by beautiful bread and pastries, left no doubts as to what we were about. The little bakery was a riot of colours, scents and sounds.

Today there are a fair few GAIL's dotted across London. We might have grown, but the way we do things hasn't changed: the best ingredients (and no preservatives), creative recipes made fresh every day, and the most important ingredient of all: plenty of time. Our original team of star bakers (Roy, Cyril, Remek, Oded, Mustapha and Raam) is still the soul of the bakery.

We're so pleased to have the chance to make good on our promise to our customers and share our bakers' secrets. After all, it's our customers who have played the greatest part in making us what we are today (along with my co-founders Ran Avidan, Gail Mejia and Emma King). When we first started out, we had no grand vision – we weren't copying a traditional French boulangarie, or indeed anything else. We were trying to create something soulful, unique and distinctive to our home city of London. It was wonderful, and it was hard. Quite honestly, sometimes we didn't have a clue what we were doing. But our customers did. They took us by the hand and guided us. They wanted sandwiches and cakes and quiches, so we made them. They wanted us to be seasonal and creative, so we changed our range regularly. They wanted us to open up in their neighbourhood, so we did.

I love that GAIL's is a part of something bigger and richer in people's lives. Don't get me wrong: we don't pretend to be doing anything grander than making great food. But I've been privileged to watch the lives, careers and families of our bakers and customers grow and flourish over the years. This is the part that I get the biggest kick from, and I hope that when you make these recipes, you're creating your own memories around a table with people you love.

Roy's recipes allow you to bring GAIL's home, no matter what your schedule is or how skilled a baker you are. If you want to invest in a (life-changing) labour of love, there's a French Dark Sourdough recipe – for us, the ultimate expression of artisan baking. Or you can knock out some cream buns on a weekend morning before an afternoon barbecue. You'll never be left wondering what to do with leftover bread again, thanks to Roy's endless ideas for turning what could be waste into something beautiful. Considering we throw away some 680,000 tonnes of bread every year in this country, that's not a bad trick to learn. The bulk of it is the sliced, plastic-packed variety, so arguably, it's not very lovable, but once you appreciate what makes an artisan loaf so special – when you've taken the time to mix, knead, shape, rise and bake your own loaf – you'll want to love, use and savour every last little crumb. And then get started on the next loaf.

Tom Molnar
Co-founder

THE ESSENTIALS

THE BAKER'S STORE CUPBOARD

A great end result depends on the best possible ingredients – whether they be seemingly basic things like flour, water and salt, or the freshest seasonal fruit and the finest chocolate. These are some of the most commonly used and more crucial ingredients that we use in the bakery.

FLOUR

The most important ingredient of all (other than time). These days most supermarkets stock a good range of bread flours. Go organic whenever you can. When it comes to flour, the confidence that organic gives you – both in terms of the product and the processing – is worth paying a little extra for, and even relatively expensive flour still won't break the bank.

Flour types aren't interchangeable. Strong bread flour has more gluten in it than plain flour, so where a recipe calls for strong flour, it's imperative to use it. Gluten is a naturally-occurring wheat protein and is what helps to give bread its structure and substance. Think of the difference in texture between a loaf of bread and a light sponge cake and you've got the idea.

With that in mind, experiment with different flours within the same flour type – a strong stoneground wholemeal, for example, will give a very different texture to your loaf than a regular strong wholemeal. Only you can say what you like best.

WATER

If at all possible, use filtered water or a still mineral water when baking. Water straight from the tap can often have a discernible chlorine taste, and, depending on where in the country you live, be too 'hard' – too full of minerals.

Water temperature is particularly important when working with yeast. Where ice-cold water is specified, it's because it will help to keep the temperature of the dough low while kneading, which keeps the yeast working at a minimum until the right moment.

Room temperature water is as warm as you should go in recipes – don't use lukewarm water to rush the process, despite what you might read elsewhere. As always, more time = more flavour.

SALT

A natural flavour enhancer, salt is a key player in the kitchen, both in savoury and sweet dishes (salt actually makes the sweet taste even sweeter). However, it also plays a more technical role in recipes where yeast is used. It helps to retard the action of yeast, helping with that slow fermentation process that's so crucial. It retains water, strengthens the gluten, and helps to create a gorgeous crust on a loaf. If you're watching your salt intake for health reasons, by all means feel free to reduce the salt in a recipe, but be aware that in some cases it may affect more than just the flavour.

If salt comes into direct contact with yeast, it will kill it, so take care when mixing both ingredients into a dough.

We use two kinds of salt. The first, fine sea salt, is used when the salt needs to be completely and evenly incorporated. The second, flaked sea salt, comes in snowflake-like crystals that are perfect for sprinkling over food, giving texture as well as flavour. We love Maldon salt. Note that both kinds are sea salt, rather than the cheaper, more processed table salt, which has an unpleasant metallic tang.

Because fine sea salt comes in much smaller particles than flaked sea salt, the same quantity takes up a much smaller space. Half a teaspoon of fine salt is as salty as a whole teaspoon of flaked salt. Try to use the kind specified in each recipe, but if you do have to make substitutions, bear this in mind. It's easy to add more salt, and impossible to take it out.

YEAST

All our recipes use fresh yeast as first preference. Fresh yeast is inexpensive and keeps for up to 10 days in the fridge. Do a bit of research to find any potential source of fresh yeast near you – it might be a deli, a grocers or, even, a bakery. It's generally sold in small pre-packaged cubes.

If you can't find it, you can use dried yeast. You need half the weight of dried yeast – as you're dealing with very small amounts, accurate digital scales will prove invaluable. You will need to follow the manufacturer's directions about reconstituting it.

BUTTER

When you see butter listed in a recipe, assume it's unsalted. That's our standard, go-to butter and what we use for almost everything. There are exceptions, and where salted butter is needed, it's specified.

Butter is such a crucial ingredient for both texture and flavour that it's worth buying the finest you can afford. At the bakery we use Lescure, made in the Poitou-Charentes region of France. With its high butterfat percentage and slight but characteristic acidity, it has a depth of flavour and a richness that's hard to match. Échiré is another top French brand.

Jersey butter, made from wonderfully leisured cows, is also amazing. If you can find good, local small producers at a deli or farmers' market (or, even, online), then support them and use their butter.

When frying with butter, add a tiny drizzle of vegetable oil to the pan to prevent it from burning.

MILK

Whole milk is best for baking. Skimmed milk, frankly, isn't worth anyone's time.

CREAM

Cream is graded according the percentage of butterfat it contains: clotted cream is the richest (somewhere between cream and butter, really), then double cream. Whipping cream is slightly less rich than double cream, and single cream is only half as rich as double cream.

Cornish clotted cream is just perfect for serving in dollops alongside a slice of cake or tart – and, of course, on scones. Double cream makes wonderfully rich custards. Single cream is good for pouring but, if we're honest, we like to serve a jug of double cream at the table too! Sour cream and crème fraîche are creams with cultures added to give them an acidic tang. We love to serve them in dollops alongside a range of sweet and savoury dishes.

The difference in quality between cream from a farmers' market or deli, where the cows are given more space and time to roam on lusher grass, and the cream on a supermarket shelf, is remarkable. Go local if you possibly can.

YOGHURT

Full-fat Greek-style yoghurt is almost always the best option. Supermarket brands are absolutely adequate, though if you live near a Greek or Turkish deli it's worth seeing what they stock.

BUTTERMILK

A tangy, thick, yoghurt-like liquid, traditionally buttermilk was the liquid left over once cream had been churned to make butter. The bacteria naturally present in the milk produced acid, giving it its distinctive flavour. These days, now that dairy products are pasteurised, buttermilk is made by introducing a culture to milk.

Either way, it's buttermilk's acidity that is so useful in recipes. You can find it in larger supermarkets and wholefood shops, but if it proves hard to track down, substitute a runny, natural yoghurt; some sour cream or crème fraîche thinned with a little milk; or, even, full-fat milk soured with a few drops of lemon juice and left to stand for a couple of minutes.

EGGS

That your eggs should be free-range goes without saying and, ideally, they should be organic too. Organic eggs have a richer flavour and a deep yellow, almost orange yolk. Above all, they come from happy chickens. Except where specified, we use medium eggs.

Eggs keep well at room temperature, although they will last a little longer stored in the fridge (also a good idea if you live in a hot climate). The temperature of eggs affects the way they behave when introduced to other ingredients. Sometimes this doesn't matter, in which case we haven't specified. Sometimes it's crucial to use either fridge-cold or room temperature eggs, so when the recipe gives one or the other, don't ignore it or you might run into problems.

SUGAR

Sugar is graded according to both the fineness of the particles and its purity. Brown sugar has more of the impurities left in, which gives it that characteristic molasses flavour. It also contains more moisture. We always opt for muscovado sugar (light or dark as required), which is less refined and less processed. If you can't find it, regular brown sugar will do.

Caster sugar, with its finer granules, dissolves more readily into other ingredients. When a sweet crunch is required, we use demerara sugar. Icing sugar is used for a final flurry to dust cakes and pastries, giving a professional finish.

HONEY

Honey stays true to its flavour throughout the baking process, so pick a fragrant, floral, high-quality clear honey: it will make all the difference.

If your honey has crystallised, stand the jar in a bowl of warm water to help it to become liquid again. Don't heat it strongly or directly or you'll damage its delicate flavour.

OLIVE OIL

We keep two types of olive oil in the kitchen – both extra virgin. The first kind is a relatively inexpensive one used for cooking – for frying, for roasting, in dough such as the focaccia, and in salad dressings where it's combined with other strong flavours. It's delicious, and well-rounded, but less precious than the second kind that we keep for drizzling and finishing dishes (or for mopping up with bread).

For those purposes – where the oil won't be heated or hidden behind other ingredients – we use the best we can possibly find. It's peppery, fresh, complex in flavour, bright in colour – and, admittedly, it's also pricey, but you only need a little at a time, and it finishes a dish to perfection. We actually find ourselves using French olive oils more often than Italian, Spanish or Greek but let your taste and preferences guide you.

RAPESEED OIL

Rapeseed oil is widely produced in the UK and is a good, home-grown, relatively neutral oil to use in cooking and baking. Sunflower oil or other neutral-flavoured oils can be substituted.

VANILLA EXTRACT AND PODS

Always buy natural vanilla extract rather than artificial essence. If you can actually see the vanilla seeds in the extract itself, it's likely to be good. Vanilla pods should be fat and juicy, which shows they contain a lot of moisture. Use vanilla pods when you need a very pure flavour (for example, when you are making vanilla ice cream or custard) and use a high-quality vanilla extract when it's part of a combination of flavours.

CHOCOLATE

Check the percentage of cocoa solids in chocolate before you buy it – it makes a huge difference. If in doubt, anything around 70 per cent will give a depth of flavour but not be overpowering or bitter. In some recipes we specify chocolate with a slightly lower percentage of cocoa solids.

COCOA POWDER

Be on your guard: cocoa powder is not the same thing as hot chocolate powder, which usually has extra sugar and milk added. For baking, you want silky-soft, rich, dark red-brown 100 per cent cocoa powder.

LEMONS

Not all lemons are created equal. Unwaxed, ideally organic, lemons are the ones you need: if you're using the pith or zest, you don't want to add wax to your recipe. Sicilian lemons are the finest of all.

Lemons (and other citrus fruit) are seasonal, and at their peak in winter. If you're using them in summer, they may well have been in storage for several months, so won't be as juicy – in this case, you may need to use more lemons to get the same quantity of juice.

You'll get much more juice from a room temperature fruit than from one cold from the fridge. Roll the whole lemon back and forth on a counter, squishing it down to release as much juice as possible before you cut it and squeeze it.

When zesting a lemon (or any citrus fruit), use the finest grater you can. (Microplane graters might seem expensive but are fantastic for this purpose, so it's worth considering buying one.) Grate off all the bright yellow skin packed with flavoursome oil, but stop before you include too much of the bitter white pith beneath.

If you need the rind, a vegetable peeler is the simplest way to remove it in neat strips without taking off the bitter white pith too.

SPICES

When it comes to spices, freshness is key. The best place to stock up is somewhere that sells a lot of them: that way, you know that the turnover is quick and the stock will be fresh. Buying whole spices and grinding them as you need them also helps ensure they're as full of flavour as possible.

For the same reason, there's no point buying vast quantities that will only go stale – better to replenish your spice collection regularly.

For the freshest spices and the best prices, it's often worth seeking out shops that serve those ethnic communities whose cooking traditionally relies upon them – the produce here tends to be better priced and fresher than you'll find in many supermarkets.

BAKING POWDER

Baking powder is a raising agent – a combination of a mild acid and a mild alkaline. When it comes into contact with liquids and heat, the two react to give off carbon dioxide, which helps batter or dough to rise in the oven. It doesn't keep forever, so check the use-by date before you start baking or you might end up with a sad, flat result.

BICARBONATE OF SODA

Bicarbonate of soda is an old-fashioned way to raise baked goods. It's an alkaline, which means it reacts with any acidic ingredients – buttermilk, yoghurt, or lemon juice, for example – to create carbon dioxide, which then helps the batter to rise. It can clump and solidify if it gets damp, so seal the container back up firmly each time.

PEPPER

Two kinds of pepper crop up in our recipes: freshly ground black pepper (coarsely rather than finely ground) is the more familiar kind, and ground white pepper.

Finely ground white pepper gives a steady, background heat. It's also used in recipes where little flecks of black pepper would spoil the look of the finished dish.

BREADCRUMBS

Breadcrumbs are a regular ingredient in and of themselves throughout this book.

There are two kinds: fresh breadcrumbs are made with day-old, slightly stale bread, crusts removed, and blitzed. Dry breadcrumbs are made in just the same way, but are then toasted in the oven to dry them out even further.

CANNED TOMATOES

A crucial ingredient in themselves, the best canned tomatoes capture all the flavour of the finest fruit and can often be tastier than watery, out-of-season fresh tomatoes. Don't waste money on tinned tomatoes pre-flavoured with herbs or other seasonings: you've no way to control the flavour or guarantee it'll be what you need for your recipe.

NUTS

Buy the freshest ones you can. Old, stale nuts taste rancid and bitter. Taste before you buy, if possible, and in small quantities so you use them up quickly.

FRUIT AND VEGETABLES

Get to know a good greengrocer if there's one in your neighbourhood – they'll know their stock, and can be trusted to recommend what's best and when. With so many of our recipes, the fruit and vegetables used are flexible. If you're out shopping and find that the exact kind specified aren't in season, or are unavailable, a decent greengrocer will help you to pick out alternatives. Alternatively, opt to buy weekly veg boxes from a local seller or online, so you get the freshest, in-season stock delivered to your door.

HERBS

If you find yourself cooking regularly with fresh herbs, considering growing your own, either in little pots or in your garden. It'll save you a significant amount of money in the long run, and you can snip off as much as you need. The potted herbs sold at garden centres or specialist plant retailers tend to be healthier and survive longer than those sold in supermarkets.

MEAT

Awareness of the importance of buying free-range chicken has grown over recent years, but it's also important to take care when buying pork. We only ever use free-range pork in the bakery, but the vast majority of pork products currently for sale in the UK aren't from free-range animals. Look out for free-range and ideally organic meat that comes from happy pigs, with room to roam and root about. Not only is it kinder, but it's much tastier. Always make sure you buy British, not imported, meat when at all possible.

THE BAKER'S TOOLS

As a cook, you'll never need to blame your tools if you stock up on basic, decent equipment from the start. It's also important to learn how to use the kit you already own to its best advantage. Much of what's listed here is inexpensive and will help you to become a neater, faster, more efficient baker, capable of producing more reliable results. If you're a regular baker, then the larger, more costly and more specialist pieces of equipment here are well worth considering.

OVEN

Even the most basic domestic oven can produce amazing results, and we tested every recipe in this book in an unremarkable, mid-range home cooker to prove it. The key is getting to know your own oven, with all its quirks and foibles. Spend a few pounds on an oven thermometer, and observe how things bake at different points and on different shelves: some ovens heat up more evenly than others, while some are far hotter towards the top.

It's usually worth rotating whatever you're baking by 180° halfway through to help achieve an even bake. The exception to this rule is when baking cakes or delicate, enriched loaves, where the sudden drop in temperature that opening the door will cause could lead them to collapse.

If your oven has a fan setting, it can prove useful for ensuring a more even temperature when baking biscuits, crackers and tarts. For yeasted breads and pastries, however, you're aiming to recreate the effect of a traditional bread oven, so a fan isn't recommended. That said, if experience suggests that your oven bakes better loaves when you use the fan setting, go with it. Every oven is different, and you know yours better than we do. You'll need to reduce the temperature by 20°C if using a fan oven.

OVEN THERMOMETER

It's amazing what liars so many domestic ovens are – telling you one temperature and actually running at something different. It's entirely possible that your oven is up to twenty degrees warmer or cooler than you think. An oven thermometer is a sound investment – they cost mere pounds and will help you get to know your own oven better, and achieve a perfect bake each time.

KITCHEN SCALES

Digital scales are the best option: relatively inexpensive, they give an invaluable level of precision that old-fashioned scales just can't match. They also save on washing up: in some recipes, you can simply stand a mixing bowl on them and reset them to zero every time you add an ingredient.

As well as using your scales to weigh out ingredients, use them to portion out dough where small, equal amounts are needed – for instance, when making cookies or buns.

HAND MIXER

A hand-held electric mixer is useful for mixing small quantities, creaming butter and sugar, whipping cream and whisking egg whites. There's no need to get a top-of-the-range brand: a relatively cheap version will do the job.

Despite the fact that many hand mixers are sold with dough hooks, don't use yours to knead bread dough or mix other heavy-duty doughs or batters: the motor just won't be up to it.

STAND MIXER

You could just about make all the recipes in this book the old-fashioned way, without a stand mixer, but some would be seriously hard work and would demand much more of your time. If you bake a lot, it's certainly worth investing in a robust well-known brand stand mixer.

FOOD PROCESSOR

Making breadcrumbs, grinding nuts, puréeing fruit, blending salad dressings and making mayonnaise – a food processor saves endless time and effort. Again, the better-quality well-known brands are worth paying for if you are going to use them often.

BAKING SHEET

When we refer to a baking sheet – and that's often – we mean a completely flat sheet of metal. They're sometimes referred to as cookie sheets, and can be found in kitchen shops. You need at least two – buy the largest size that your oven can hold, so that you can maximise oven space when you bake.

BAKING TRAY

These are trays that go inbetween your oven racks. They are shallow, rectangular metal tray with a slightly raised rim or lip around the edge. The dishes we use are 20cm x 30cm.

BAKING DISH

Also referred to as a pie or pudding dish. Many of the puddings and savoury dishes in this book are baked in a baking dish – a deep, rectangular, oven-proof dish.

The actual material it's made from doesn't matter: we love the classic blue-and-white enamelled baking dishes, which are inexpensive, simple but beautiful enough to serve from directly at the table.

BAKING STONE

You can produce great bread without a baking stone, but if you bake regularly then it's a highly recommended purchase that will take your loaves to the next level. Baking stones aren't particularly pricey, last forever, and will actually save you energy, as they capture the heat of the oven and intensify it directly towards your loaf. Most department stores and kitchenware shops now stock them.

WATER VESSEL

Creating steam inside the chamber of the oven is essential in many recipes. It prevents a hard crust from forming too early on the bread, and allows it to expand to its rightful size. The best way to achieve this is to toss ice cubes (or very cold water) into a pre-heated water vessel, sat on the hot oven floor, just before you shut the oven door for the final bake. There's no need to buy a specific piece of equipment for this: you can use any small baking tin or casserole.

CAKE TINS

Non-stick bakeware is almost ubiquitous now, and by far the best option. Not only does it make your life easier, it lasts longer. Silicon bakeware is best avoided except in a few very specific cases, such as our rum baba recipe (see page 240): it doesn't conduct heat properly, and your cakes won't bake as evenly, nor develop the same delicious golden exteriors that metal cake tins give.

Round springform cake tins – those with loose bottoms released with a clasp – are almost always preferable to solid-based ones. They reduce the risk that your cake will come out of its tin in pieces. One of the few exceptions to this rule is when making upside-down cakes or puddings, where the sauce would leak out if you were to use a springform tin.

Take care to wash and dry your cake tins carefully after each use to prevent them from rusting.

Throughout this book we use the following tins: a 20cm diameter springform tin; a 20cm solid-based tin, and two sizes of loaf tin – 19cm x 8cm (450g) and 24cm x 10cm (900g).

TART AND TARTLET TINS

Loose-based metal tart tins will make getting a finished tart out of its tin and onto a serving plate infinitely easier.

We use a tart tin 24cm in diameter as standard throughout this book. As we love our tartlets particularly dainty and bite-sized, most tartlet recipes use solid-based, smooth edged, 5cm diameter tins. Slightly larger, loose-based, fluted tins 9cm in diameter will also prove useful.

MUFFIN TINS

In the bakery we actually use popover tins to make our muffins, rather than traditional muffin tins. Lined with paper cases, they produce tall muffins with puffed, mushroomed tops. Popover tins are much more common in America, but can be found quite easily online. If you can't get hold of them, regular muffin tins will work just fine – your muffins will still taste as great, but they just won't look exactly like ours.

We also use regular muffin tins for baking buns and pastries other than muffins. Mini muffin tins are also useful for certain recipes.

MEASURING SPOONS

It might be fine for stirring your tea, but a regular teaspoon won't cut it when it comes to baking – the same goes for a standard tablespoon. Put them back in the drawer and buy a proper set of measuring spoons instead: you can find these cheaply and easily in kitchenware shops and supermarkets. Technically, a teaspoon is 5ml and a tablespoon 15ml. Unless specified, measure out level spoonfuls, not heaped ones.

GRATER

The most common reason for using a grater in our kitchen is to zest citrus fruits. A standard grater will do the job, but a fine Microplane grater will change your life. They're pricier but brilliant, getting the job done much more quickly and with less effort and making grated fingers (always a minor risk) easier to avoid.

A good grater will also come in handy for grating nutmeg, cinnamon sticks and hard cheeses such as Parmesan.

COOKIE CUTTERS

Metal biscuit cutters are, generally, cheaper than plastic ones. To preserve them and prevent them from rusting, never immerse them completely in water – simply wipe them clean and then dry thoroughly. There are so many wonderful and wacky shapes available: collecting them can become addictive...

DOUGH SCRAPER

One of the most useful tools a baker can possess, and priced at mere pence – you'd be mad not to buy one of these. A dough scraper will prove handy for cleaning surfaces, cutting dough, scraping down the sides of a bowl, and goodness knows what else.

BAKING PAPER

Non-stick baking paper reduces mess, protects your bakeware and helps prevent sticking. Don't confuse it with waxed paper, which is a very different thing and can't be substituted. Either the white or the more environmentally friendly, unbleached brown baking paper will do.

BALLOON WHISK

A balloon whisk is the best way to quickly whisk by hand, whether you're whisking egg whites or combining dry ingredients in recipes where sifting them isn't necessary. It's also good for whipping small amounts of cream, where over-whipping is always a potential risk: this is much easier to avoid if you're working by hand than with an electric mixer.

ROLLING PIN

We prefer French-style rolling pins – that is, the kind without handles on each end. A wooden pin (rather than the more expensive marble kind) is all you need.

PALETTE KNIFE

A palette knife has a long, broad, completely flat blade, and is used for spreading fillings, icings and toppings. It will also come in handy for levering things up and checking underneath to see that they're baked right through. If you make and ice a lot of cakes, consider buying a medium-sized angled palette knife. These are specifically designed for achieving a perfectly neat finish on cakes and tarts.

SIEVE

Sifting together dry ingredients with a fine sieve is a crucial step in certain recipes. It aerates them, removes any lumps, and gives a lighter and more risen result. A sieve will also remove lumps, pips or seeds from a coulis, purée or sauce.

PASTRY BRUSH

Don't bother with silicon brushes – a traditional wooden and bristle brush is best. Wash and dry very thoroughly after each use.

WIRE COOLING RACK

Warm bread, cakes or cookies fresh out of the oven will cool faster if the air can circulate all the way around them. A wire rack allows this to happen as well as preventing steam from building up underneath, which would create a soggy base.

A NOTE ON TECHNIQUES

MIXING AND KNEADING BY HAND

A stand mixer fitted with the dough hook will help enormously with mixing and kneading large batches of dough, and there's no shame whatsoever in using one to help you, as our recipes direct. That said, it's good to learn to do this by hand – sometimes, there are times in a recipe where a brief knead by hand is best, or perhaps you don't have a stand mixer. There's also a lot to be said for getting to know and understanding your dough by taking the time to work with it directly.

Kneading is a way of developing the gluten present in the flour. A protein, gluten can be worked, stretched and shaped into strings right at the molecular level, and it's this that gives dough its springy elasticity.

1. To mix the dough, pour the flour onto the worktop or into a bowl and form a crater in the centre. Into this, add all the wet ingredients – for example, water and sourdough starter – along with the yeast. Sprinkle the salt around the edge of the crater.

2. Use the fingers of one hand or a wooden spoon moving in small circular motions to mix together the yeast and wet ingredients, gradually pulling in more and more flour from around the edge of the well. Increase the size of the circular motions and keep going until you've mixed in all the flour. You'll have a very soft, sticky, messy lump.

3. Next, lightly flour your work surface. If the dough is sticky, that's all part of the process: don't try to get around this by adding extra flour to the dough or surface at this stage.

4. Flour your hands very lightly. With the dough in front of you, place the fingers of your less dominant hand just under half way up the lump of dough to hold it in place. Use the heel of your other hand to push the dough above your first hand firmly away from you, stretching it out to a full arm's length if you have the space.

5. Use this same hand to scrape up the stretched-out dough and gather it back to form a lump again. Rotate the dough a quarter-turn. Repeat the stretching process, working as quickly as you can. The dough will become less sticky and turn into more of a workable ball as you go.

6. After several turns, once the dough is workable, form it into a ball to keep things neat. To do this, pull the edges of the dough out and into the centre, pressing them down with your fingertips, and rotating it roughly an eighth of a turn as you go until all the edges have been brought in. Then flip the dough over, so you have a smooth, seamless surface on the top.

7. Place your hands either side of the ball, palms up, one hand towards the back of the ball and one towards the front. The edge of your little fingers and the inside edge of your palms should be touching the dough. Draw your hands together under the dough, moving the front hand towards the back and the back hand to the front. As you do this, the dough will spin slightly. Repeat this 3 or 4 times.

8. Continue to knead, forming a ball every now and then to keep the dough manageable, until you can stretch it out thinly between your hands without it splitting. It is now smooth and elastic, ready to shape and prove.

FORMING A BLOOMER

This method of shaping a loaf gives the bread a particular spring as it rises and bakes, creating the bloomer's characteristic curved shape. Here is a simple, quick technique for forming neat and beautiful loaves, it's well worth mastering.

1. Flour the worktop and your hands.

2. Take the portion of dough and flatten it into a rough oval.

3. Fold the top half of the dough down to the middle and press down, then repeat with the bottom half, creating a slight overlap. Seal this with the heels of your hands to create a seam that runs from left to right across the dough.

4. Fold the whole of the top half of the dough right over the bottom half and seal.

5. Turn the dough over so that this seam is hidden along the bottom, then prove according to the recipe.

6. Using a sharp knife cut a slash about 1cm deep along the length of the loaf before baking.

FORMING ROLLS AND BUNS

Plenty of recipes in this book call for you to shape dough into little buns or rolls. There's a simple knack to forming smooth, neat balls of dough before you leave the buns to rise, and learning these tricks of the trade will give you a gorgeous end result every time.

1. Begin with a scrupulously clean worktop (not floured) and very, very lightly floured hands. Roll the dough into a rough log and use a sharp knife or dough scraper to divide it into the number of pieces the recipe calls for.

2. Take a piece of dough and sit it on the worktop, then hold your hand just above it, palm facing down towards the work surface. Cup your palm and fingers very gently around the piece of dough, almost like a claw.

3. Begin to roll the dough around on the surface using your cupped hand, making small, circular motions – as if you were gently polishing something precious – without exerting any downwards pressure on the dough. You don't want to squash it or flatten it onto the surface.

4. As a ball begins to form, use your thumb to gently spin the dough around within your cupped hand, carefully and gradually smoothing and tucking the edges underneath as you go.

5. Continue until you end up with a neat ball of dough that looks completely 'sealed' – i.e. it has no obvious seams or cracks in it, just one, single, smooth upper surface.

6. Set on a baking sheet lined with non-stick baking paper and repeat with all the remaining dough, then prove according to the recipe.

BLIND-BAKING

Blind-baking means baking a tart case without its filling. You do this whenever the pastry requires longer baking time than the filling. It ensures that the pastry is crisp and cooked through before the wet custard, fruit or vegetables go in, avoiding the dreaded soggy bottom – few things are more crushing than a tart with flaccid, pale pastry. This crucial step also prevents the sides of the tart case from collapsing as it bakes. Different kinds of pastry will cook at different speeds, but the technique is always the same. Keep a close eye on each tart case to get the cooking time right. You're aiming for fully-cooked, ready-to-eat pastry. Baking beans are available from kitchenware shops. They weigh pastry down, so it doesn't puff up in the oven. They're also designed to conduct heat evenly. If you don't have any, you can use dried pulses or rice. The pastry should be well-chilled to prevent it from becoming sticky and difficult to handle. If it becomes too soft, put it back in the fridge to firm up.

METHOD

On a lightly floured surface, roll out the pastry to a 3mm-thick disc, just slightly larger than the size of the tart tin you're using. (The recipes in this book make tarts 24cm in diameter.) Push the rolling pin from front to back, a few times, then turn the dough a quarter-turn, and roll away from you again. Shift the pastry around on the surface, flip it over from time to time, and add a little extra flour if necessary to prevent sticking. When it's fully rolled out, dust off any excess flour with a pastry brush.

Place the tart tin right in front of you, lightly wrap the pastry around the floured rolling pin, then lift the rolling pin and allow the pastry to unroll right into the tin. Press the pastry gently down into the base of the tart tin, making a neat, sharp angle between the sides and the base of the tin, but don't push or stretch it too much. If you stretch it now, it will shrink when baked. Gently press the pastry evenly up the sides of the tin, then use a knife to trim neatly all around the top. The tart case should be exactly level or almost imperceptibly higher than the tin you're using.

Chill for at least 30 minutes. Meanwhile, preheat the oven to 180°C/gas mark 4. Line the case with sturdy foil or non-stick baking paper and fill it with baking beans. Bake for 15–20 minutes until the outer edge is done. The centre won't be quite ready yet. Remove from the oven, allow to cool until you can handle it, then carefully remove the beans and foil. Return to the oven and bake for 10 minutes more, until the pastry is an even golden colour and completely cooked through. Sweet pastries will turn a slightly darker golden shade than savoury ones because of their sugar content. Remember that, even if your recipe requires a second stage of baking, the case won't colour further.

Allow the case to cool completely before filling.

BASIC RECIPES

CRUMBLE TOPPING

Ours is an unorthodox approach to crumble, not in terms of the ingredients – which couldn't be simpler or more typical – but in the method. Sandy, dusty, coarse crumble is a sad thing to see and eat, and adds little in terms of flavour or texture. To avoid that, we push our mixture further than most, rubbing the butter into the flour well past the point you might expect. This forms little nuggets almost of shortbread or buttery biscuit among the crumbs, which highlights the flavour of the butter and makes for a gorgeous, crunchy texture that provides a genuine contrast to whatever fruit, cream or dough lies underneath. For added crumbliness we dry the crumble out in the fridge for at least an hour, or ideally overnight, so it's best made a day in advance.

METHOD

Put the flour and butter in a bowl and use your fingertips to rub the butter into the flour (you also can do this using a mixer fitted with the beater attachment) until the mixture resembles breadcrumbs. Add the sugar and continue until you're left with large crumbles – distinct nuggets of buttery dough should form. Don't be afraid to really go for it and work the dough, pressing and rubbing it together between your fingertips.

Spread the crumble out on a plate or baking sheet lined with baking paper and chill for at least an hour in the fridge, or overnight. Don't cover – the cold air in the fridge will help to dry it out and make it even crumblier. It will keep for 3–4 days.

INGREDIENTS

150g plain flour
100g salted butter,
     chilled and diced
50g caster sugar

Makes: 300g

FLAKY FROMAGE FRAIS PASTRY

Making genuine, full-blown flaky pastry is a time-consuming business. Luckily for us (and you!), we've perfected a recipe that gives the same light, buttery, crumbly result and takes 10 minutes flat. It can be subbed for flaky or traditional shortcrust pastry in almost every situation.

METHOD

Put the flour, cold butter and salt in a large mixing bowl. Using your fingertips or the beater if using a stand mixer, rub the butter into the flour until you have something that looks like coarse breadcrumbs, with a few larger specks of butter left here and there (these will add to the flaky texture).

Add the fromage frais all in one go and mix until combined. The dough will be sticky, but don't overwork it or your pastry will be tough. Form into a rough ball, flatten out on cling film into a rectangle, wrap and chill for at least 2 hours, or overnight, then use as required.

INGREDIENTS

250g plain flour
250g butter, chilled and diced
1 tsp fine sea salt
175g fromage frais,
    sour cream or full-fat
    Greek-style yoghurt

Makes: 1 large tart, about
    20cm x 30cm

SWEET ALMOND PASTRY

Pastry made with sugar will always be slightly more delicate than savoury versions. The addition of ground almonds makes a particularly delicious, short pastry. That said, this recipe is not only quick to make, it is also relatively easy to work with and can be depended upon not to shrink in the oven. It forms the base of many of the sweet tarts in this book, and the almond flavour works exceptionally well with fruit.

METHOD

In the bowl of a stand mixer, beat the butter with the beater until light and creamy. Stop the mixer, scrape down the bowl, then add 100g of the flour, the icing sugar, the ground almonds, the egg and the salt. Mix at medium speed until a soft paste forms, then stop and scrape down the bowl. Add the rest of the flour and mix until just combined.

Wrap in cling film, press to create a disc and chill for at least 2 hours, or ideally overnight before using, or store for up to 3 days in the fridge until needed, then roll out and bake according to the recipe.

INGREDIENTS

220g butter, at room
    temperature
380g plain flour
140g icing sugar
55g ground almonds
1 egg, plus 1 egg yolk
½ tsp fine sea salt

Makes: 860g, enough for 2 tarts
    24cm in diameter

PASTRY CREAM

Pastry cream – also known by its French name, crème pâtissière – is one of the pastry chef's most useful tools and crops up regularly throughout this book. Essentially a thick milk-based custard stabilised by the addition of cornflour and usually flavoured with vanilla, it's far more dependable than plain whipped cream. Once prepared, it makes a near-instant filling for tarts – the perfect base for fresh fruit. It's also traditionally used to fill éclairs and profiteroles.

Pastry cream takes a few hours in the fridge to set and develop the right consistency, so is best made a day in advance. But if you keep it for much more than a day, its texture will deteriorate.

METHOD

Split open the vanilla pod lengthwise with a sharp knife and use the edge of the blade to scrape out the seeds. Put the pod and seeds into a small, heavy-based saucepan along with the milk and the sugar.

In a separate bowl, whisk the egg yolks and cornflour until pale in colour.

Heat the milk and sugar mixture until just boiling, stirring regularly. Gently and very slowly, pour it onto the yolks – just a dribble at first – while you whisk constantly with a balloon whisk. When all the milk has been added to the yolks and is whisked in well, strain through a fine sieve and back into the saucepan. Keep the vanilla pod and return it to the pan. Over a low heat, stir the pastry cream until it thickens into a custard. Once it starts to bubble, cook for 2–3 more minutes, stirring all the time.

Pour into a clean bowl and cover with cling film, pressing the film right down so that it touches the surface of the pastry cream – this is a handy trick that prevents a skin from forming. Chill for at least 1 hour before using, or overnight.

INGREDIENTS

½ vanilla pod
250ml milk
50g caster sugar
3 egg yolks
20g cornflour

Makes: 250ml

EGG WASH

A modest little recipe this, but one that crops up again and again. Brushing the surface of pastry with beaten egg yolk helps it to develop a deep golden colour and a rich gloss. You only need a little at a time, but it will keep, covered, in the fridge up to two days, to be used as and when.

METHOD

In a small bowl, use a fork to beat the yolks with the salt until completely smooth and blended. Cover and chill until needed.

INGREDIENTS

2 egg yolks
a pinch of fine sea salt

TOASTING NUTS

A toasted nut is a tastier nut: exposure to heat amplifies all the sweetness and richness of their flavour. There's virtually no kind of nut that won't benefit from a spell in the oven before being used in a recipe. When appropriate, we like to keep the skins on for maximum flavour and goodness.

Different nuts take varying lengths of time to toast, but they can all go from just perfectly done to bitter and burned in a matter of seconds, so need careful monitoring. Nuts with a very high fat content (macadamia nuts, walnuts and pine nuts – not technically nuts, but seeds) require closer attention and slightly less time than other varieties.

Preheat the oven to 180°C/gas mark 4 and spread the nuts evenly on a baking tray in a single layer.

Toast in the oven until they just begin to catch the faintest hint of colour, then stir and move around on the tray to ensure the nuts all cook evenly.

Put back in the oven for a few more minutes. Your nose is as much of a guide as your eyes in judging when they're ready – the nuts should be beautifully fragrant, but not smell acrid or bitter. Larger nuts such as hazelnuts and almonds will take roughly 10 minutes in total, pine nuts barely 4–5 minutes.

When properly toasted, the insides will have changed colour slightly as well as the outside. Cut into a couple to check. Taste only once cooled, as it's impossible to judge the flavour while the nuts are still hot.

Allow the nuts to cool completely before chopping or blitzing, or they'll turn to an oily mess.

MAYONNAISE

Homemade mayonnaise knocks the socks off your average big brand versions, though you can now find very good quality ready-made mayos in delis and some supermarkets. It's actually very simple indeed to make and you shouldn't be afraid of trying it. We like our mayonnaise quite tangy, so we add a fair amount of lemon juice and some Dijon mustard. Throughout this book, mayonnaise is often mixed with other ingredients to create flavoured versions, and these ingredients help it to hold up well. If you prefer your mayo plainer, you can reduce the quantities of lemon juice and mustard.

There's no need to use extra virgin olive oil in mayonnaise, save it for your alioli. Neutral flavoured rapeseed oil (or other vegetable oil) is what's needed to make a dressing that will support but not overpower whatever you serve it with.

You can make mayonnaise with a food processor, a balloon whisk, or with a hand blender – the kind usually used for blending soup. If using the latter, there's a cunning trick you can use to make the process even easier (see below). Homemade mayonnaise will keep for 2–3 days in the fridge.

METHOD

If using a food processor or working by hand, blitz or whisk the yolks together with the lemon juice, mustard and salt. As you continue to mix, start to add the oil drop by drop at first, then in a slow but steady stream. Continue until all the oil is completely incorporated and you have a glossy, creamy mayonnaise. If the end result is a little too stiff and jelly-like, add a few drops of water to let it down – this is particularly useful if you're planning on using your mayonnaise in a salad dressing.

If using a stick blender, simply combine all the ingredients except the oil in a measuring jug or cup. Pour the oil on top and leave to settle for 30 seconds, then put the head of the stick blender right at the bottom of the jug and start blending. This will create a vortex, gradually sucking the oil down into the other ingredients and forming a mayonnaise. Slowly tilt the head of the blender up as this happens to suck in more oil until everything is combined. It should take no more than a minute.

Cover and chill until needed.

INGREDIENTS

3 egg yolks
2 tbsp lemon juice
1 tsp Dijon mustard
1 tsp fine sea salt
200ml rapeseed or other
    neutral-flavoured oil

Makes: about 300g

GAIL'S KETCHUP

This ketchup is best known and loved in our bakeries as the accompaniment to our Sausage Rolls (see p.130), but it's also useful for making barbeque sauce for the Pulled Pork Sandwiches (see p.154). It's much less sweet than shop-bought brands, which leaves more room for the flavour of the tomatoes themselves to shine through. It'll keep for weeks in the fridge in a sterilised glass jar or bottle (to do this either run your container through the dishwasher on a hot wash, then immediately fill with ketchup, or put 4 tablespoons water in the jar and microwave on full power for 2 minutes). Carefully tip out the water (it will be boiling) and dry upside down on kitchen paper.

METHOD

Mix all the ingredients in a large pan and bring very slowly to the boil. Reduce the heat to very low, and simmer gently for 3 hours, until reduced by half. Leave to cool completely, then pour into a sterilised bottle or jar and tightly seal.

INGREDIENTS

700ml passata
180ml white wine vinegar
40ml dark soy sauce
70g light brown sugar

Makes: 500ml

HOUSE SYRUP

Our wonderful chef Asher gets the credit for this recipe. Originally we wanted to serve our French toast and pancakes with maple syrup, but then we thought about making our own syrup – after all, we already make our own ketchup, brown sauce and dips. For us, the ultimate syrup would taste just like the caramelised juices that run out of a tarte tatin when it bakes. With that in mind, this is what we came up with: the most amazing syrup on the planet. It's worth making a big batch because it keeps forever in the fridge, and is great with yoghurt, ice cream and all manner of things, as well as on French toast or pancakes, of course.

METHOD

Begin by making a caramel. In a large pan, combine the sugars in an even layer. Over a low heat, without stirring, cook the sugars until they begin to melt in places, then swirl the pan to help them dissolve more easily. Continue to cook until the sugars have dissolved, then watch like a hawk as it turns into dark amber caramel, just at the point where it's about to start smoking.

As soon as the caramel is a dark amber, add the spices, the vanilla pod and seeds and the diced apple – the pan will splutter slightly – and stir in well. Cook until the apples are soft – about 10 minutes. Carefully add the water in three batches, stirring well, then bring the syrup back to the boil and simmer for 20–30 minutes, until reduced by half. You'll be left with a dark, syrupy liquid.

Remove from the heat and strain through a fine sieve into a clean heatproof container, pushing the apple pieces and spices against the sieve to extract as much flavour as possible. Cool to room temperature then cover and store in the fridge.

INGREDIENTS

150g caster sugar
200g demerara sugar
8–10 cardamom pods, crushed
    under the blade of a knife
    to open them slightly
3 cinnamon sticks
2 vanilla pods, split lengthways
    and seeds scraped
150g (about 2) cored, peeled
    Bramley apples, cut into
    2cm cubes
700ml water

Makes: about 450ml

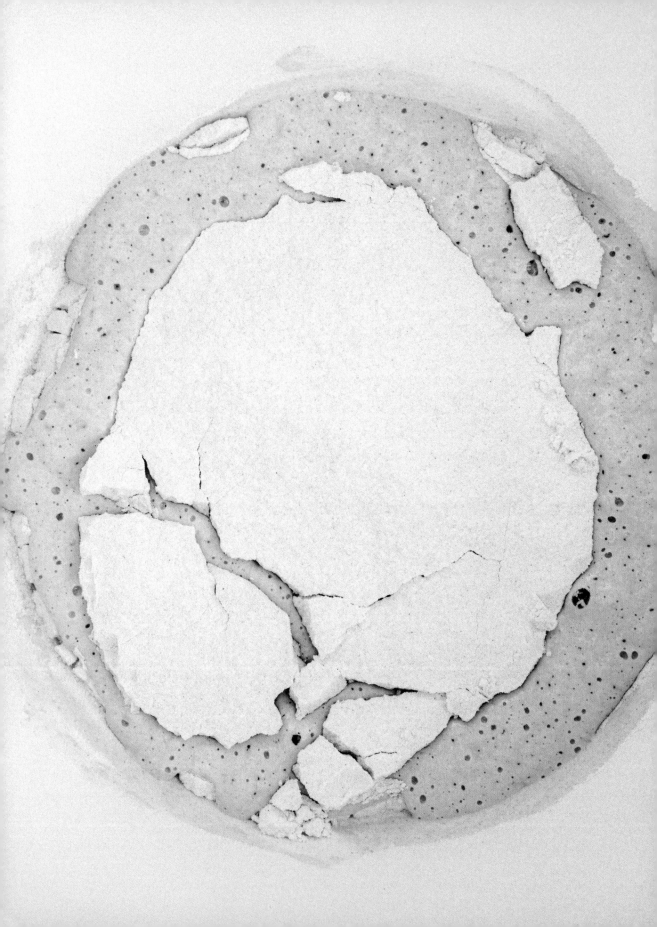

BREADS

FRENCH DARK SOURDOUGH

Sourdoughs are the mother lode of bread-making, with more and more bakers looking to this traditional method to instruct and inspire them. This is how bread is meant to be. From the characteristic, holey, chewy texture to the rich chestnut crust and, above all, the complex, tangy flavour, a sourdough loaf is simply in a different league to the long-life, pre-sliced, plastic-wrapped 'breads' to which we've all become accustomed.

For centuries, natural leavens were at the heart of every domestic kitchen. Nobody could see the yeast cells or understand their part in the process, but people knew that something was there in the initial mix of water and flour and that, given time, it made dough rise. Today, we know that wild yeast cells are all around us – on every surface and in the air – and they are all seeking to land on a nice, nourishing food source for their next meal. Once they find something good to eat – like a sourdough starter – they will feed, multiply and produce carbon dioxide. (A bit like us, then, really!)

This is as low-tech as you can get. Baking with sourdoughs might be bang on trend now but, once upon a time, this was the only way. Sourdough, old dough, biga or mother dough: these are all different terms for the same thing – the leavens that make the difference between a well-risen loaf with a defined structure of crust and crumb, and a flat pita bread.

Of course, good ingredients are crucial to great bread – but they're far from the whole story. Dough is a living creature, and it reacts to everything around it: temperature, humidity, the touch of your hand, the mechanics of the mixer and, most importantly, time. Slowing down the process by lowering the temperature of your dough is a trick that good bakers use, and one you'll learn here. If you hear someone talk about slow fermentation, this is what they mean. Keeping the dough as cold as possible for as long as possible prevents the yeast from working too quickly. It begins with mixing the dough with ice-cold water, and continues with keeping the dough as cool as you can over as long a period as possible before the final proving and then baking.

When it comes to baking your bread, everything's turned on its head. You want the hottest oven possible, and this trial by fire will put the final stamp on your loaf.

The first stage is to make a starter, which will take at least ten days. You'll then need to begin making the loaf itself the day before you want to bake and eat it: allow around 4 hours to mix, prove and shape the dough, a resting period overnight in the fridge, an hour the next morning to reach room temperature, then an hour to bake and cool (see p.46 for photograph).

THE STARTER

A sourdough starter is the living heart of traditional baking. Making your own is challenging to start with, but once you get the hang of it, your sourdough will become your faithful kitchen companion. If you look after your starter – feeding it, watering it – it will reward you in turn. Use this starter for all the sourdough recipes in the book.

METHOD

Mix the first day's ingredients in a very clean small bowl with a scrupulously clean fork until you have a solid, stodgy batter. Pour the starter into a clean plastic container at least four times its volume and cover it loosely with a lid so it still lets in a little air. There are yeast cells all around and, hopefully, some of them will latch on to this mix. Put the starter in a cool room – but not in the fridge, a cupboard, or any other enclosed space. After one day, feed the starter for the first time. Weigh out 150g of the starter and discard the rest. Feed the remainder with the 70g of wholemeal flour, 20g of strong white flour and 75ml water. Put back in its container and cover it loosely. Leave it to rest for another day.

Repeat each day, for 10 days or ad infinitum – literally. Your sourdough could live for ever, unless you forget to feed it – in which case it will die. If you're going away for a few days, you can move it into the fridge, where the cooler temperature will slow down the work of the yeast and allow it to survive for two days without you. Be sure to bring it back to room temperature before its next feed.

It will take between 7–10 days for your mixture to grow into a vigorous sourdough starter. As time passes, you should see that something is happening. It should bubble gently more and more with every passing day, and the smell should be fresh and yeasty, with a hint of alcohol. If the scent is unpleasant, with sour, vinegary notes, throw it away and start again – unfortunately, this is a sign that the wrong bacteria have colonised it.

After 10 days, if both you and your starter are happy, together you're ready to make the loaf of your life – a loaf that is the cornerstone of every artisan bakery in France and beyond. Weigh out your 150g to keep feeding as a starter and, instead of discarding it, use the rest to bake sourdough bread.

If you don't have a stand mixer, see p.27 for mixing and kneading by hand.

Continued overleaf

INGREDIENTS

For the starter:
120g strong wholemeal flour
20g strong white bread flour
120ml water, at room temperature

For feeding over 10 days:
10 x 70g strong wholemeal flour
10 x 20g strong white bread flour
10 x 75ml water at room
   temperature

THE BREAD

METHOD

Combine the flours in a stand mixer bowl with the salt. Add the ice-cold water and knead slowly with the dough hook for 10 minutes. Now add the starter and continue to knead on low speed for 5 minutes. Increase the speed to medium-high and knead for another 6 minutes. The dough should be fairly firm and still cool to the touch.

Take the dough out of the bowl, place it on a clean, lightly floured surface, and knead (see p.27 for more on kneading technique) it with the heel of your hand for a few minutes.

Let the dough rest: return it to the mixer bowl, cover the bowl with damp, clean tea towel and let it rest at room temperature for 1½ hours. Knock it back with your hand to let out all the air that will have built up inside, cover the bowl with the cloth and rest it again for another 1½ hours before punching the air out of it again.

To shape your loaves, cut the dough in half on a floured surface. Shape each piece in turn, pressing it down with your fingers to form a rough, plump disc. Pull the edges into the centre of the disc, piece by piece, then turn the dough over. You should have created a tight, neat ball of dough with a tense surface. Repeat with the second portion of dough.

Rest the dough again. Line a baking sheet with non-stick baking paper and dust it generously with flour. Carefully place the loaves onto this, spaced well apart to allow room for them to rise. Dust a little more flour and place a sheet of baking paper on top. Place the whole thing in a plastic bag roomy enough to cover them loosely. Inflate the bag so that it won't come into contact with the dough.

Place on the warmest shelf in the fridge (usually at the top), and leave to rest for 8–10 hours, or overnight. Slow, cold fermentation is crucial to developing the full flavour and fragrance of a well-made loaf.

When fermented, remove from the fridge and place them – still wrapped – on the worktop, well away from any draughts. This next stage is all about gentle warmth and bringing the dough up to room temperature (around 20°C). Depending on how hot your kitchen is, this could take an hour, or more. Once it reaches room temperature the dough will become active and you should check in on it every 30 minutes to see how it's doing until doubled in bulk. Poke the dough with your finger: it should feel like a slightly deflated balloon, but should spring back easily.

INGREDIENTS

440g strong wholemeal flour
50g strong white flour
2½ tsp fine sea salt
350ml ice-cold water
150g sourdough starter
whole tray of ice cubes

Makes: 2 small (500g) loaves

Preheat the oven to its highest setting, then place a baking stone or baking tray on the middle shelf to heat up. Place a small baking tin on the oven floor to act as a water vessel and let this heat up as well.

Uncover the loaves and let them breathe while the oven is heating. When ready to bake, take a razor-sharp knife, angle it at 45° to the dough and score four long incisions around 1cm deep in a square on the top of the loaf. As well as helping to create a beautiful loaf, these cuts serve a useful purpose: they allow the bread to expand evenly as it bakes.

To bake the bread, carefully pull the oven rack with the hot baking sheet or stone halfway out of the oven. Working as quickly as you can, gently slide the loaves onto the hot surface, spaced apart but close to the centre, and push the rack back into the oven. Tip all the ice cubes into the tin at the bottom of the oven and close the oven as swiftly as possible. The cloud of steam that develops inside the oven stops the crust from seizing up as the dough hits the heat, allowing the bread to expand and develop. It will also help to give you a crisp, shiny crust. After 10 minutes, reduce the heat to 200°C/gas mark 6 for a further 30 minutes.

When the bread is fully baked, turn off the oven, open the oven door slightly and leave the bread in the oven for a further 5 minutes to let off some steam – quite literally. Transfer to a wire rack to cool. This cooling down period is a crucial part of the baking process, and can't be rushed, no matter how impatient you are to taste your bread. Leave the bread for at least an hour before you slice it and dig in.

ONION SEED SOURDOUGH

This loaf has all the flavour and character of a sourdough, but with a little extra fresh yeast to help it along. It's intensely savoury, and is great with strong cheese, rich stews or soups. You'll need to begin the day before you want to bake: allow around two hours to mix, prove and shape the dough, a resting period overnight in the fridge, an hour the next morning to reach room temperature, then an hour to bake and cool. If you don't have a stand mixer, see p.27 for mixing and kneading by hand.

METHOD

Combine all the dough ingredients in the bowl of a stand mixer and knead with the dough hook for 4 minutes. Add the flavourings, increase the speed to medium, and mix for 10 minutes more. Remove the bowl from the mixer, cover with a clean, damp tea towel, and leave to rise for an hour. Use your fists to punch out excess air, then turn onto a floured surface. Halve the dough and form each portion into a bloomer loaf (see p.28 for how to form a bloomer).

Line a baking sheet with baking paper and dust with flour. Transfer the loaves onto it, then put inside a large plastic bag, inflated so that it won't come into contact with the dough. Place in the fridge and leave to prove for 8–10 hours, or overnight.

When proved, place the loaves – still wrapped – on the worktop to come up to room temperature (around 20°C). Depending on how hot your kitchen is, this could take an hour, or more. Once at room temperature check on them every 30 minutes until they have has doubled in bulk. Poke the dough with your finger: it should feel like a slightly deflated balloon, with plenty of air still inside it but not on the verge of popping. Watch after you poke it: it should spring back easily.

Place a baking stone or baking sheet on the middle shelf and preheat the oven to its highest setting. Place a small baking tin on the oven floor to act as a water vessel. To finish the loaves, brush with water and dust thickly with extra flour. Cut a slash about 1cm deep down the length of each one.

To bake, carefully pull the oven rack with the hot baking sheet or stone halfway out of the oven. Working quickly slide the loaves onto the hot surface, and push the rack back into the oven. Tip the ice cubes into the tin at the bottom of the oven and close the oven as swiftly as possible. After 10 minutes, reduce the heat to 200°C/gas mark 6 for a further 30 minutes. When the bread is baked, turn off the oven, open the door slightly and leave the bread for 5 minutes to let off some steam. Transfer to a wire rack to cool for at least an hour before you devour it.

INGREDIENTS

For the dough:
2g fresh yeast
350ml ice-cold water
150g sourdough starter
25g strong wholemeal flour
500g strong white bread flour

For the flavouring:
3 tsp fine sea salt
3 tsp nigella seeds
3 tsp sesame seeds
30g black onion seeds

For finishing:
a little water
strong white bread flour,
    for dusting
whole tray of ice cubes

Makes: 2 small (500g) loaves

FRUIT AND NUT SOURDOUGH

Here's a relatively quick recipe – if your sourdough starter is ready to use, you're only three hours away from freshly baked loaf. This makes some of the best toast ever. It's also great served with strong cheeses. If you don't have a stand mixer, see p.27 for mixing and kneading by hand.

METHOD

Combine all the dough ingredients in the bowl of a stand mixer and knead with the dough hook for 10 minutes on low speed. Add the flavourings and continue to mix on low speed for 5 minutes more.

Remove the bowl from the mixer, cover with a clean, damp tea towel, and leave in a draught-free spot at room temperature to rise for an hour.

Turn the dough out onto a floured surface and shape into a round loaf. Line a baking sheet with baking paper, dust with flour, and transfer the loaf onto it. Slip the whole thing into a large plastic bag, inflated so that it won't come into contact with the dough. Leave to rise at room temperature for 1½ hours, until doubled in size. Poke the dough with a finger: it should feel like a slightly deflated balloon, still full of air but not about to pop. After you poke the dough, check that it springs back quickly into shape.

Preheat the oven to its highest setting, then place a baking stone or baking sheet on the middle shelf to heat up. Place a small baking tin on the oven floor to act as a water vessel.

Brush the top of the loaf with water, dust thickly with the flour, and slash a cross into it with a sharp knife, making your incisions 1cm deep.

To bake the bread, carefully pull the oven rack with the hot baking sheet or stone halfway out of the oven. Working as quickly as you can, carefully slide the loaf onto the hot surface, and push the rack back into the oven. Tip all the ice cubes into the tin at the bottom of the oven and close the oven as swiftly as possible. The cloud of steam that develops inside the oven stops the crust from seizing up as the dough hits the heat, allowing the bread to expand and develop. It will also help to give you a crisp, shiny crust. After 15 minutes, reduce the heat to 200°C/gas mark 6 for a further 25–30 minutes.

When ready, turn off the oven, open the oven door slightly and leave the bread in the oven for 5 minutes to let off some steam. Transfer to a wire rack to cool for at least an hour before you devour it.

INGREDIENTS

For the dough:
5g fresh yeast
200ml ice-cold water
150g sourdough starter
250g strong white bread flour
40g strong wholemeal flour

For the flavouring:
120g walnuts halves
120g sultanas, soaked in
    boiling water for 15 minutes,
    then drained well and
    squeezed to remove any
    excess water
1½ tsp fine sea salt

For finishing:
strong white bread flour,
    for dusting
whole tray of ice cubes

Makes: 1 large (800g) loaf

WHITE POPPY SEED BLOOMER

Somewhere in the vicinity of hardcore sourdough, wild yeast and prayer sits this ingenious method for generating a *poolish* (to use the French terminology) that will leaven your bread with virtually guaranteed results. This *poolish* is generated with the help of baker's yeast, but other than that, nothing here is different from the classic sourdough technique. This is sourdough light, if you will, but only in how you make it – not in flavour. And don't let anyone look down their nose at it. It's as bona fide as any sourdough and does the job magnificently. If you don't have a stand mixer or food processor see p.27 for mixing and kneading by hand. Start the bread the day before you want to bake it (see p.47 for photograph).

METHOD

First make the *poolish*. Take a small container with a lid and mix all the ingredients until you have a smooth batter. Cover loosely with the lid and place in the fridge overnight. You should find it bubbling gently the next morning – a sure sign that the yeast is working.

Place the flour, water and yeast in the bowl of a stand mixer and mix for a couple of minutes with the dough hook until you have a smooth mixture. Add the *poolish* and knead on slow speed for 8 minutes, then add the salt. Increase the speed to medium and continue kneading for 6 minutes.

Cover the bowl with a clean, damp tea towel and leave to prove at room temperature. Once the dough has doubled in size, turn it out onto a floured surface and punch it back with your fists to knock out the air. Halve the dough – you'll notice that this is very soft and sticky, so don't be afraid to use plenty of extra flour as you work. Knead each piece lightly by hand into a bloomer shape. You can do this by flattening it into a cushion shape and rolling it tightly into a bloomer (for how to form a bloomer, see p.28), or you can use the play-dough method, just shaping it as best you can. Always remember, this is home baking, not championship competitive sport, and what counts above all is taste.

Line a baking sheet with baking paper. Flour it well. Place the loaves on the sheet, well apart and place in a large plastic bag, inflated so it does not touch the dough. To bake today, prove for about 1 hour until doubled in size and bake as below. To bake tomorrow, place the loaves in the fridge to prove slowly. Remove them several hours before you want to bake them, as proving from a very cold temperature takes much longer. Place them on the worktop, and allow them to double in size.

INGREDIENTS

For the *poolish*:
375ml water
380g strong white bread flour
10g fresh yeast

For the bread:
830g strong white bread flour
375ml cold water
5g fresh yeast
25g fine sea salt
poppy seeds, for sprinkling
whole tray of ice cubes

Makes: 2 large loaves,
about 1kg each

When proved, preheat the oven to 220°C/gas mark 7, with a baking sheet or stone heating up on the centre rack, and an empty pan at the bottom to hold ice cubes to create steam. Remove the loaves from the plastic bag, still on their tray. Lightly brush or spray the surface of the dough with water to help the poppy seeds to stick then scatter the poppy seeds generously over the loaf. Using a sharp knife cut a slash about 1cm deep down the length of each loaf.

Carefully slip the loaf onto the hot surface, and tip the ice cubes into the bottom pan. Quickly shut the oven door and bake for 30-40 minutes, until the crust is a dark golden brown. Turn off the oven, open the oven door a little, and leave it in the oven to let off some steam. This should take another 5 minutes. Cool on a wire rack a little before tucking in.

VARIATIONS: To make breadsticks, simply form small lumps of dough and then roll them out on a floured surface to long, thin pencils of dough – as thick or thin as you like. Lay on a baking sheet – no need to prove – and brush with a little olive oil, sprinkle over some salt, seeds, herbs or spices as you prefer, then bake in an oven preheated to 220°C/gas mark 7 until crisp – around 20-25 minutes.

To bake a pull-apart loaf, form half the dough into 20 little 50g buns. Sit them in a baking dish measuring about 30cm x 40cm and between 3-4cm deep, forming 4 rows of 5 buns. Leave to prove inside a well-inflated plastic bag at room temperature until they have risen to fill the dish, and are all touching – about an hour. Brush with olive oil and sprinkle with salt, grated cheese, or herbs, as you prefer. Bake at 220°C/gas mark 7 for 25-30 minutes until puffed and golden. Put the whole loaf at the centre of the table for everyone to dig into.

WHOLEMEAL LOAF

When it comes to bread, the French are right about a lot of things – but they were wrong when it came to wholemeal. They became obsessed with white flour as a status symbol and this obsession elevated the art of white bread-making until it came to symbolise the nation. What could be more French than the baguette? While we all adore a well-made baguette, there's something irresistible about the scent of wholemeal bread. It's as if the smell of soil and dried, harvested fields of wheat is brought to the plate through the scent of the baked flour. Wholemeal bread in general has a slightly denser structure – it isn't as frivolous or ephemeral as white bread. And the butter in the recipe? Everything tastes better with butter, say we. If you don't have a stand mixer, see p.27 for mixing and kneading by hand.

METHOD

Place the water, flour, yeast and butter in the bowl of a stand mixer and knead with the dough hook on a low speed for 10 minutes. Then add the salt and knead for another 5 minutes.

Take the bowl out of the mixer and cover with a clean, damp tea towel. Place well away from draughts until doubled in bulk – about 1–2 hours. Lightly butter or oil a 24cm x 10cm loaf tin. When the dough is ready, turn it out onto a floured surface and punch it down with your fist.

Knead by hand for a couple of minutes, gradually forming it into a pillow shape roughly as wide as the tin. Roll it into a bloomer (see p.28) as long as the tin without letting any air pockets form. Place in the tin, seam side down. Put the loaf inside a large plastic bag, inflated so that it won't come into contact with the dough, and leave to rise, well away from any draughts, until doubled in size again – around 1–2 hours.

Alternatively, to bake tomorrow, place the covered tin in the fridge and let it rest overnight. This will do wonders for the flavour of the bread. Remove from the fridge at least 2 hours before you plan to bake and allow to come back to room temperature. When the dough shows signs of life monitor it until it has doubled in size.

When proved, preheat the oven to 220°C/gas mark 7 and put a small baking tin on the base of the oven to act as a water vessel. Use a pastry brush to gently moisten the top of the loaf with water and sprinkle the oats on top. Tip the ice cubes into the baking tin and sit the loaf on the centre shelf. Bake in the oven for 30–40 minutes until well-risen with a dark brown, rounded, crusty top.

Remove from the oven and turn out of the tin immediately. Return to the oven for a further 10 minutes to dry out the crust. Transfer to a wire rack to cool before slicing.

INGREDIENTS

400ml cold water
560g stoneground
    wholemeal flour
15g fresh yeast
20g butter, at room
    temperature
2 tsp fine sea salt
handful of rolled oats,
    for topping
whole tray of ice cubes

Makes: 1 large loaf

CHOLLA

Recipes transcend borders. No matter where you are in the world, come Friday, if you're Jewish, then there's a good chance that there will be a cholla bread on your dining table. It's blessed before the Friday night family dinner as part of a tradition of giving thanks for being alive, and having food to eat. If you don't have a stand mixer, see p.27 for mixing and kneading by hand.

METHOD

Combine the yeast and water in the bowl of a stand mixer and stir with a fork until completely dissolved. Add the flour, sugar, eggs and olive oil. With the dough hook, mix on a low speed for 5 minutes to combine. Add the salt and increase the speed to medium for a further 8 minutes. Remove the bowl from the mixer and cover it with a clean, damp tea towel. Leave the dough to rise, well away from any draughts, until it has doubled in size – about 1½–2 hours. Turn the dough out onto a lightly floured surface. Use your hands to punch the air out of it and divide it into thirds. Take each piece in turn, and roll it back and forth to stretch it into a long thin roll about 50cm long.

Now you're ready to braid. Take your three logs and press them together at the end furthest away from you, with the central strand pointing directly towards you and the other two roughly at 90° from each other. Cross the right strand over the central one, laying it gently in the space between the central log and the left strand. What was on the right is now in the centre. Lift the left strand over the central log, placing it in the space between the central and right logs. Repeat until the braid is complete.

Line a baking sheet with baking paper and carefully transfer the cholla onto it. Slip the whole thing into a large plastic bag. Inflate the bag so that the dough doesn't come into contact with the plastic. Leave to prove again for 1½–2 hours, depending on the temperature of your kitchen. The loaf should be visibly larger, though not doubled in size.

Meanwhile, preheat the oven to 200°C/gas mark 6. Lightly brush the top of the loaf with egg wash, making sure it goes into every fold and crevice. Sprinkle the seeds on top and place in the centre of the oven. Immediately reduce the heat to 180°C/gas mark 4 and bake for 40–45 minutes. Halfway through baking, rotate the baking sheet from front to back to ensure an even bake. The finished cholla should be a glossy, chestnut brown. Cool on the tray for 10–15 minutes before transferring to a wire rack to cool completely.

VARIATIONS: Use brown sugar or honey in place of the sugar for a more mellow, caramel flavour.

INGREDIENTS

20g fresh yeast
200ml cold water
550g strong white bread flour
100g caster sugar
3 eggs
4 tbsp olive oil
1½ tsp fine sea salt
egg wash (see p.35)
2 tsp sesame seeds
2 tsp poppy seeds
fine sea salt

Makes: 1 loaf

SPELT ROLLS

Ancient wheat and other native food plants are a constant source of wonder. Spelt is a relic, and all the better for it – this is the wheat that time forgot. The few farmers who grow it in this country did an incredible job of bringing it back to the attention of the bread-baking public, and we now know what a true champion spelt is, compared with the much more common hybrid, wheat. You'll find spelt flour in the usual guises of white and wholegrain, just like any other flour and it can – and should – be used as you would any other flour.

These rolls are just the ticket for a lazy weekend morning, provided you plan and begin a day ahead – and are not all that lazy the day before. If you don't have a stand mixer, see p.27 for mixing and kneading by hand.

METHOD

Combine the flour, yeast, honey or sugar and the water into the bowl of a stand mixer, and knead with the dough hook for 7 minutes at low speed. Add the salt and knead for 3 minutes. Remove the bowl, cover with a clean, damp tea towel, and allow the dough to rise for 1½–2 hours at room temperature until almost doubled in size.

Turn the dough out onto a lightly floured surface and knead it into a log shape. Using a sharp knife or a dough scraper, divide the log into 16 rolls, each weighing around 40–45g. Shape them into little balls (see p.30 for how to form rolls). Line a baking sheet with baking paper and dust with flour, then place the rolls on it and place the whole thing inside a large plastic bag, inflated so that it won't come into contact with the dough. Allow to rise once more at room temperature, for 1½–2 hours, until doubled in size. When they are nearly ready, place a baking stone or another baking sheet in the oven and heat the oven to 200°C/gas mark 6. Place a smaller baking tin on the oven floor to act as a water vessel.

Dust the rolls with a little more flour and make a snip halfway through the middle of each one with a sharp pair of scissors. Before putting the rolls in the oven, tip the ice cubes into the pan on the bottom. (This will help to form a better crust.) Quickly take the baking stone out of the oven and in one swift motion, slide the baking paper with the rolls on it onto the hot stone. Place the rolls in the centre of the oven and bake for 13–15 minutes until the bottom of the rolls are golden brown. They should open up like little tulips as they bake. Transfer to a wire rack to cool for 10–15 minutes.

INGREDIENTS

450g wholegrain spelt flour
10g fresh yeast
30g honey or caster sugar
300ml cold water
1½ tsp fine sea salt
whole tray of ice cubes

Makes: 16 little rolls

CREAM BUNS

Simplicity is the essence of bread-making, and here's a recipe that reminds us of that. These little buns are deliciously soft and ever so slightly sweet, and thanks to the cream and the butter in them, they're rich on the palate, with a tender crumb. They make the cutest and most luxurious sandwiches for a party or for a child's packed lunch and can be served with pâté, cured meats, strong cheese, soups and salads – almost anything. If you don't have a stand mixer, see p.27 for mixing and kneading by hand.

METHOD

In the bowl of your stand mixer, use a fork to whisk together the yeast and milk until the yeast dissolves. Add the eggs, cream, sugar, flour and butter. Knead with the dough hook at low speed for 5 minutes to bring the ingredients together into a dough. Add the salt and increase the speed to medium for a further 6–10 minutes, until the dough looks silky and starts to pull away from the sides of the bowl.

Take the bowl out of the mixer and cover with a clean, damp tea towel. Leave it to sit on the worktop for 1 hour or until the dough has doubled in size.

Turn the risen dough out onto a floured surface and cut it into 22 pieces weighing around 50g each. Shape them into little balls (see p.30 for how to shape buns). Place the buns onto a baking sheet lined with non-stick baking paper and slip it inside a large plastic bag, inflated to stop the bag touching the surface of the dough. Leave to rise again for another 1–1½ hours until doubled in size.

Preheat the oven to 190°C/gas mark 5. Gently brush the surface of the buns with egg wash. Sprinkle over the poppy seeds or sesame seeds mixed with a little sea salt. Bake them in the oven for around 10 minutes until they are golden in colour and their bases are cooked through – lift one with a palette knife to check. Cool on a wire rack.

VARIATIONS: For extra texture and crunch, dust the rolls with semolina or polenta instead of the seeds. For a fruity version, add 35g sultanas and 25g fennel seeds to the dough itself, at the same time as you add the salt.

TO FREEZE: If you don't want to bake all the rolls at once, freeze them once shaped, on a baking sheet, wrapped in cling film. They'll keep for up to a week. Defrost them overnight in the fridge, then leave to come to room temperature for 1½ hours, then prove and bake as above.

INGREDIENTS

For the buns:
15g fresh yeast
50ml milk
3 eggs
150ml double cream
70g caster sugar
500g strong white bread flour
100g butter, diced and at room
    temperature
1½ tsp fine sea salt
egg wash (see p.35)

For the topping:
2 tsp poppy seeds
2 tsp sesame seeds
1 tsp flaked sea salt

Makes: 22 little rolls

FOCACCIA

Focaccia can be made quickly and be fresh on the table in just a couple of hours. Or you can take it slow, as we do at GAIL's, and give it that extra oomph that comes from a long fermentation – but the truth is that warm bread served straight from the oven, glistening with olive oil, will be a winner whichever route you take. You don't even have to wait for this to cool down before you rip it apart. If you don't have a stand mixer, see p.27 for mixing and kneading by hand.

METHOD

Sift the flour into the bowl of a stand mixer and add all the remaining dough ingredients. Knead with the dough hook on a slow speed for 8–10 minutes until smooth, soft and elastic.

Place the dough in an oiled bowl, swivelling it inside the bowl until it is coated with oil on all sides. Cover with a clean, damp tea towel and leave to rise at room temperature. After 45 minutes, punch the risen dough back with your fist, re-cover with a damp, clean tea towel and leave for another 45 minutes, punch down again, then repeat a third time.

Let the dough rise one last time. Lightly oil a deep baking tray or roasting tin measuring about 27cm x 30cm. With your fingers, gently coax the dough into a flat shape to cover the tray. This will only work if the dough is relaxed enough to push around. If it shows signs of wanting to spring back to its original form, leave it to relax for another 10 minutes and try again. The surface should be nicely cratered with your finger marks – this is what gives focaccia its characteristic dimpled surface.

Give the dough another 20 minutes or so to rise a final time while you preheat the oven to 200°C/gas mark 6. Drizzle olive oil generously all over the focaccia, and sprinkle on the rosemary and sea salt to taste. Bake in the oven for 10 minutes, then reduce the heat to 180°C/gas mark 4 and continue to bake for a further 15 minutes until cooked right through but still soft and pillowy. Check that the base is golden brown and fully baked, even in the centre. As soon as you take the focaccia out of the oven, drizzle over yet more olive oil and serve immediately.

TO MAKE IN ADVANCE: If you'd like to save the focaccia to bake the next day, place it inside a plastic bag, inflated so that it won't come into contact with the dough, then chill overnight. Remove and allow it to come to room temperature and rise a little before baking – around 1½ hours in total.

INGREDIENTS

For the dough:
500g strong white bread flour
    (plus a little extra for dusting)
330ml cold water
50ml extra virgin olive oil (and
    a little extra for greasing)
2 tsp fine sea salt
10g fresh yeast
45g clear honey

For the topping:
olive oil, for drizzling
2 sprigs of rosemary, needles
    only, chopped
flaked sea salt, for sprinkling

Makes: 1 focaccia

IRISH SODA BREAD

We're fully paid-up students of the school that says that time and patience are as important to good bread as top-quality ingredients. But then there's Irish soda bread, a loaf legendary the world over, which takes almost no time at all. The process is so quick and straightforward that this must be the easiest real bread to make at home. It's even all made by hand – no appliances need apply. Ah, the luck of the Irish…

Use black treacle for a stronger flavour or golden syrup or clear honey for a milder flavour.

This bread is meant to be enjoyed as soon as it is cool enough to slice, with lashings of butter. It doesn't keep for more than a day (at a push, you can toast it thoroughly the next day). But when fresh, it's delicious with smoked fish or fresh oysters. And did someone say ham?

METHOD

Preheat the oven to 200°C/gas mark 6 and place a baking stone or baking sheet inside to get hot.

Sift all the dry ingredients into a large mixing bowl. Stir together the wet ingredients in a separate mixing bowl and add them to the dry, mixing with a wooden spoon. Now it's time to get your hands dirty. Holding the bowl with one hand, use your other hand to knead the dough in the bowl until you feel that everything is well combined. The finished dough will feel slightly tacky and sticky. Don't overwork, though, or the loaves will be tough.

As soon you can, bring the dough together into a ball, turn it out onto a lightly floured surface and divide into two equal parts. Form these into two balls. Sift a little extra flour over the dough. Take a sharp knife and cut a deep cross into the top of each ball, deep enough to go down through half the height of each loaf. Quickly remove your hot baking surface from the oven and place the loaves on it, spaced well apart. Replace in the centre of the oven and bake for 40 minutes until dark and crusty. Cool briefly on a wire rack and serve whilst still warm, ideally.

INGREDIENTS

250g wholemeal flour
250g plain flour,
    plus extra for dusting
1½ tsp fine sea salt
4 tsp bicarbonate of soda
350ml buttermilk
30g treacle or golden syrup
4 tsp rapeseed oil

Makes: 2 small loaves,
    450g each

SEEDED BUTTERMILK AND TREACLE LOAF

Don't be put off by the lengthy list of ingredients. This is a batter bread: as easy as stirring a pot, and as rewarding. It has such powerful umami flavours that sometimes we're left asking ourselves whether it's a bread or a cake.

The recipe came to us via a South African friend. In South Africa this loaf is eaten like us Brits eat scones.

This amazing loaf is really an invitation to experiment. But do stick to this flour combination: it works. Excellent with smoked fish, cheeses and salads – oh, and it makes the best egg salad sandwich. A note on the treacle: black treacle would give you a strong flavour. Golden syrup or honey will give you a milder flavour.

METHOD

Preheat the oven to 170°C/gas mark 3 and grease and line a 19cm x 8cm loaf tin with baking paper.

To make the bread, mix together the flours, baking powder, salt, oats and mixed seeds in a large bowl. In a separate bowl, stir together the buttermilk, treacle and rapeseed oil until combined. Add the wet mixture to the dry and stir with a wooden spoon until evenly combined. The result should be more of a batter than a dough.

In a separate bowl, mix together the topping ingredients.

Pour the dough into the greased loaf tin and tap the tin lightly on the worktop to level the batter. Sprinkle the salt and seed mix over, and bake for 1 hour or until the centre springs back when lightly pressed.

Cool in the tin for about 15 minutes, then turn out onto a wire rack. This bread must be completely cold before slicing. It keeps brilliantly, and can be stored in an airtight box for a few days.

INGREDIENTS

For the bread:
55g strong white flour
55g strong wholemeal flour
1 tsp baking powder
1 tsp fine sea salt
40g rolled oats
1 heaped tbsp sesame seeds
1 heaped tbsp pumpkin seeds
1 heaped tbsp linseeds
1 heaped tbsp poppy seeds
1 heaped tsp nigella seeds
175ml buttermilk
50g treacle or golden syrup
4 tsp rapeseed oil

For the topping:
1 tsp rolled oats
1 tsp sesame seeds
1 tsp nigella seeds
1 tsp sunflower seeds
1 tsp pumpkin seeds
1 tsp linseeds
1 tsp poppy seeds
½ tsp flaked sea salt

Makes: 1 loaf

BRIOCHE LOAVES

Walking into the bakery early in the morning when brioche is baking is one of the greatest moments in a baker's day. It means wafting on a cloud of cooked, sweet butter. It's like stepping into cake. The scent sticks to your clothes and stays with you all day. If bread is good and bread and butter is better, then brioche has to be best of all.

We love brioche in its own right, especially toasted with plenty of jam, but it's also a steppingstone towards so many more dishes, both sweet and savoury. Toasted slices of brioche are perfect with pâtés, or slip slices under poached eggs smothered with Hollandaise for an indulgent Eggs Benedict. If the loaf is a few days old – a little dried up and lonely – that's your cue to turn it into bread and butter pudding, or French toast. Plenty more recipes in this book call for brioche dough so, if making this recipe, you might choose to use half to make a brioche loaf, and put half to another use.

METHOD

With a fork, whisk together the yeast and milk in the bowl of a stand mixer and leave to sit for a few minutes. Add the flour, eggs, sugar and half the butter. Knead with the dough hook at low speed to a soft dough for 3–4 minutes. With the machine running, start to add the rest of the butter, one lump at a time. When it has all been incorporated, increase the mixer speed to medium and continue to knead for another 6–8 minutes. When the dough starts to pull away from the sides of the bowl, add the salt and increase the speed to fast. Continue mixing until the dough is shiny, smooth and elastic.

Remove the bowl from the mixer and cover with a clean, damp tea towel. Leave at room temperature to rise for 1½–2 hours, or until the dough has doubled in size. Then, use your fist to knock the dough down inside the bowl to take the air out of it. Cover the bowl in cling film and put in the fridge to rest overnight. (If you are using this to make another recipe that calls for brioche dough, this is the stage that you need to reach.)

The next day, butter two loaf tins measuring 24cm x 10cm. Divide the dough in half and form them into smooth, rounded bloomers. Sit them snugly inside the tins, cover and leave for a couple of hours to come back to room temperature and to double in size. When nearly ready, preheat the oven to 190°C/gas mark 5. Lightly brush the tops with egg wash, slash the loaves three times lengthways with a sharp knife and bake for 30–40 minutes. The entire top crust should have turned into a dark, glossy bark. Leave to cool for 10–15 minutes then remove from the tin and cool on a wire rack.

INGREDIENTS

20g fresh yeast
2 tbsp milk, at room temperature
500g strong white flour
5 eggs, at room temperature
50g sugar
250g salted butter, at room temperature (plus an extra 50g to grease the baking tins)
2 tsp fine sea salt
egg wash (see p.35)

Makes: 2 large loaves

BREAKFAST

CROISSANTS

A good, handmade croissant is a thing of wonder. It's often said that the real test of a baker is the ability to make a croissant. Whereas bread succumbs to the baker, the baker succumbs to the croissant. If you do decide to put the time and effort into making these, you'll be well rewarded with a sublime combination of texture, flavour, aroma and colour. Their success hinges partly on the technique and partly on the quality of butter you use: try to find sweet, unsalted French butter, with a high fat content. (See our notes on ingredients at the front of the book.)

This dough is also used to make several other recipes in this chapter, so if you want, you can use half of it for croissants, and half for something else. As so often, the most important ingredient of all is time, and you'll need to allow a full day to make these – though, of course, you won't be working on them all the time, you will be able to do other things in between!

METHOD

Before you do any baking, make a template for cutting the croissants. Out of a piece of reasonably stiff paper or card – a cereal box or magazine cover will do nicely – cut a triangle with a 12cm base and two equal 20cm sides.

To make the dough, mix the yeast, water and 150g of the plain flour with a wooden spoon in the bowl of a stand mixer to create a thick paste. Sift over the remaining 200g plain flour in a thick layer, and leave to sit for 15–20 minutes, until you can see the flour beginning to crack as the yeast works underneath it. Add the strong flour, butter, sugar, salt and milk, and knead on a slow speed using the dough hook for 5 minutes, until you have a soft but not completely smooth dough.

Tip the dough out of the bowl onto a clean surface and knead by hand for a few more minutes, forming it into a ball. Lightly flour a rolling pin and press the dough out into a rectangle measuring 20cm x 30cm x 5cm. Transfer it onto a baking sheet lined with non-stick baking paper, wrap it well in cling film, and freeze for 30 minutes.

While the dough chills, take the butter for laminating the dough out of the fridge and leave it to warm up for 15 minutes. Put it into a sandwich bag or between two pieces of plastic film and press it down to create a rectangle of butter, about 15cm x 20cm and 1.5cm thick. Chill until the dough is ready.

Continued overleaf

INGREDIENTS

For the dough:
40g fresh yeast
200ml cold water
350g plain flour
750g strong white bread flour
110g butter, at room temperature
80g caster sugar
25g fine sea salt
350ml milk

For laminating the dough:
600g butter, chilled

For glazing:
egg wash (see p.35)

Makes: 18 large croissants

Roll the chilled dough into a long rectangle, 15cm x 60cm. Lay it in front of you on the largest surface you have, short edges at the side and long edges at the top and bottom. Press the chilled butter over the right side of the rectangle, then fold the left half on top of it, as if closing a book. Press the dough out with the rolling pin, working away from you, front to back only, not side to side – the direction you roll in is absolutely crucial. Create a rectangle that's 1cm thick, and 1 metre long. One long side should be the folded edge, sealed up, the other should be open.

Mentally draw two lines across the long rectangle stretched out in front of you, dividing it into thirds. Fold the bottom third up, then the top third down over that, rather like folding a letter. Transfer the folded dough back to the baking sheet, wrap in cling film and freeze for another 30 minutes.

Remove from the freezer, unwrap, and sit the dough in front of you exactly as it was before, like a folded letter, then give it a quarter turn so that the long edges are at the sides and the short edges at the top and bottom. Roll it out again a rectangle 1 cm thick, and 1 metre long. Mentally draw a line half way up the dough, then fold the bottom edge up to meet the centre line, and do the same with the top edge. Finally, fold the entire top half of the dough back down over itself. Return to the baking sheet, wrap, and freeze for 30 minutes more.

Remove from the freezer, again, and position it in front of you so that the long edges are at the sides. Roll from front to back to create a 40cm x 60cm x 5mm rectangle. Turn the dough again so that the short edges are at the sides, then cut in half, from left to right to give two oblongs, 20cm x 60cm.

Each strip of dough will give 9 croissants, plus a few leftover pieces. With a large, very sharp knife and your stencil, cut out triangles of dough. Don't drag the blade through the dough: press it down into it in one motion to avoid stretching out the layers you've created.

Shape the triangles into croissants; hold the base of the triangle in one hand and stretch the tip away from it very slightly, to elongate it into an Eiffel tower shape. Start to roll the dough up from the base to the tip, then lay each croissant, tip tucked underneath, onto a baking sheet lined with non-stick baking paper, leaving 5cm in between each croissant. You'll need two baking sheets. The best place to prove the croissants is in a completely cold oven. Put them on the centre shelf, along with a small bowl of hot water on the floor of the oven, and shut the door. Leave for 2 hours, until risen and springy to the touch – they won't double in size. Remove from the oven along with the bowl of water. Preheat the oven to 200°C/gas mark 6.

Brush the tops of the croissants lightly with egg wash, being absolutely careful not to brush the cut sides of the croissants, with their exposed layers, or you won't get a flaky result. Place in the oven and immediately reduce the heat to 180°C/gas mark 4. Bake for 20–25 minutes, until a very deep, golden brown. Don't risk under-baking them. To test, lift one up carefully and ensure that the base is an even, dark gold. Your entire kitchen will smell of baked butter. Eat them within a few hours.

TO MAKE IN ADVANCE: If you want fresh croissants for breakfast – and you probably do – you can chill the shaped baking sheets of croissants overnight, covered in cling film. Just allow them to come to room temperature for 30 minutes or so, then unwrap, prove and bake as above.

TO FREEZE: Once the croissants are shaped, you can cover them in cling film and freeze for up to a week. Leave them in the fridge to defrost overnight, then on the worktop for an hour to come to room temperature, prove in the oven and bake as above.

ALMOND CROISSANTS

So what happens at the end of the day, when any leftover croissants bite the dust? The short answer is they go to heaven, and re-emerge the next morning as something which is much, much more than the sum of its parts – a divinely decadent almond croissant. We're always looking for ways to get crafty with leftovers, and limit waste. Luckily the same attitude is a big part of traditional French baking, and the almond croissant – soaked in syrup, filled with almond cream, crisply caramelised around the edges and gooey inside – is its ultimate expression.

If you have a food processor, grind the almonds freshly yourself. If you don't, you'll need to use shop-bought, ready-ground almonds. These are easily available, but give a slightly muted texture and taste – though you'll still end up with an excellent result.

It is important the croissants are stale and dry, so they can absorb as much syrup as possible. Leave them out in a paper bag overnight, not in plastic in the fridge or a bread bin.

METHOD

Make the almond cream: in the bowl of a stand mixer fitted with the beater, or by hand with a wooden spoon, beat the butter until soft and creamy. Add the sugar and continue to beat until pale and fluffy. Add the almonds, mix in thoroughly, then add the eggs one by one, beating well each time.

In a separate bowl, mix together the flour and the cornflour, then add this to the butter mixture and blend until smooth and there are no lumps left. Cover the bowl tightly with cling film or spoon into a container with a lid. Chill in the fridge for at least an hour.

To make the vanilla syrup, heat the caster sugar, demerara sugar and water in a pan over a medium heat. Gently bring the contents to the boil, then reduce the heat and simmer for five minutes until the liquid is syrupy. Stand the base of the pan in a bowl of cold water for several minutes, stirring occasionally, until comfortably warm but not boiling hot, then stir in the vanilla.

Meanwhile, preheat the oven to 170°C/gas mark 3. Cut each croissant along the side of its belly using a serrated knife. Dip them in the warm syrup one at a time, and allow to soak for 5 seconds. Gently press each syrup-soaked croissant between your palms to let a little of the liquid drain away. Drenching the croissants in syrup stops them from burning when baked for the second time, and helps to turn the flaky layers of pastry within into a soft, melting centre.

INGREDIENTS

8 plain croissants, 1–2 days old and as dry as possible

For the almond cream:
200g butter, at room temperature
200g caster sugar
200g whole almonds, skins left on, coarsely ground in a food processor so that a few nibs of almonds are left unground (or use ready-ground almonds)
3 eggs, at room temperature
30g plain flour
30g cornflour

For the vanilla syrup:
250g caster sugar
250g demerara sugar
500ml water
1 tsp natural vanilla extract

For the topping:
80g flaked almonds
icing sugar, for dusting

Makes: 8 large croissants

Place the soaked croissants on a baking sheet lined with non-stick baking paper, open up the slit in their sides, and fill them with almond cream – they should hold about 3 generous tablespoons. Seal them back up, spread another tablespoon or so of almond cream on top, and sprinkle over the flaked almonds.

Bake for 30 minutes. Test them by inserting a knife between the croissant and its almond cream filling. If the filling has puffed up and is thoroughly cooked, your croissants are ready. Leave to cool for 10 minutes, then dust with icing sugar and serve.

TO MAKE IN ADVANCE: The almond cream can easily be made a day (or two) in advance, covered and chilled. You can also prepare the croissants right up to the baking stage, then cover with cling film and chill for up to two days. They can go straight from the fridge into the oven, but might need a minute or two longer to bake. Or you can just make the filling a day or two in advance (but don't add the cherries until ready to bake) cover and chill in the fridge.

TO FREEZE: If you want to make the almond cream up to two weeks in advance, it freezes well. Just defrost overnight in the fridge and beat it thoroughly to bring it together before using it.

FRUIT DANISH

Our take on Danish pastries adds another dimension of texture and flavour to the soft pastry and gooey filling – a crisp, candied almond topping. Once you've mastered croissant dough, this is another chance to put it to great use with very little extra effort required. Here, we suggest you use plums but you can use any fresh stone fruit, or figs, poached pears, or apples and/or raisins.

METHOD

Lightly butter 9 tartlet tins, each 9cm in diameter. Roll the chilled croissant dough into a 30cm square, 5mm thick. Cut it into 9 10cm squares: use a long, sharp knife, and don't drag it through the dough – cut it by pressing the blade down into the dough with a single motion.

Sit each square in a tartlet tin and press the dough down very gently, then prove the dough: put the tartlet tins onto a baking sheet and place on the centre shelf in a completely cold oven. Put a small bowl of hot water on the floor of the oven and shut the door. Leave the pastries for 2 hours to prove, without opening the oven.

Make the topping: in a small bowl, beat the egg white with a fork until foamy. In a separate bowl, stir together the flaked almonds, the icing sugar, the vanilla, and a little of the egg white to act as glue – add just enough to bind the nuts with the sugar.

When the pastries have proved, take the tartlet tins out of the oven and preheat it to 200°C/gas mark 6. Lightly brush them with egg wash. Drop a tablespoon of pastry cream in the centre of each one, leaving a decent margin around the edge. Top with the sliced plums, and sprinkle the topping around the edge onto the exposed pastry. Put into the oven, immediately reduce the temperature to 180°C/gas mark 4 and bake for 20–25 minutes until a rich golden brown, with a toasted, crunchy almond topping, and juicy, almost bursting fruits. Best served warm.

TO MAKE IN ADVANCE: The formed squares of dough, in their tartlet tins, can be put on a baking sheet, wrapped in cling film, and chilled overnight in the fridge. Leave them out for 30 minutes to come to room temperature, then prove and bake as above.

TO FREEZE: The squares of dough can be frozen in their tartlet tins, well wrapped in cling film, for up to a week. Transfer them to the fridge to defrost overnight, then on the worktop for an hour to come to room temperature, before proving in the oven and baking as above.

INGREDIENTS

For the pastries:
butter, at room temperature, for greasing
½ quantity croissant dough (see p.66), after the final rolling out
1 quantity pastry cream (see p.34)
9 ripe, juicy plums, stoned and cut into wedges
egg wash (see p.35)

For the topping:
1 egg white
120g flaked almonds
50g icing sugar
1 tsp natural vanilla extract

Makes: 9 Danishes

CINNAMON BUNS

This twist on croissants came to us from California. They're a West Coast invention, and weren't often seen this side of the pond. Certainly, we'd not come across them until our friend Kit Williams showed us how to make them in the early days of GAIL's, and it's no exaggeration to say that our lives haven't been the same since. Croissant dough works spectacularly in pains au chocolat, pains aux raisins and Danish pastries. But cinnamon buns take the biscuit.

Americans are obsessed with the flavour of cinnamon, but, actually, their preferred spice is cassia (which they call cinnamon). It has a stronger aroma and flavour than 'true' cinnamon and the bark is also thicker and tougher. There's one variety which comes from Vietnam and is particularly superb. We were blown away when Kit introduced us to it. It was love at first sniff. If you can get someone to bring you some from the States, do try it. As with so many other ingredients, until you are confronted with the finest quality, you don't understand how good they can be. We're always learning. For the record, cinnamon and cassia are interchangeable in any recipe: it's all a matter of preference.

METHOD

First, make the croissant dough to the last rolling out. Butter one or two muffin tins with a total of 14 large cups, greasing the flat surface between the cups as well as the cups themselves.

Next, make the filling: mix together the muscovado sugar, caster sugar and cinnamon until combined and set aside.

On the most spacious kitchen surface you have, roll the chilled croissant dough out to a 30cm x 80cm rectangle, 3–4cm thick. Lay it out in front of you so that the short edges are at the sides.

Use a pastry brush to brush the dough with melted butter, leaving a 4cm-wide border along the top long edges. Sprinkle the filling all over the melted butter, and pat it down so that it begins to dissolve into it.

Starting from the long edge closest to you, roll the dough up tightly, like a Swiss roll. Turn it so that it's sitting on its seam. With a sharp, non-serrated knife, slice the log of dough into 14 equal buns. Take each bun and tug the loose end of the rolled dough out to stretch it very slightly, then tuck it under one of the cut ends of the bun to seal it up – this creates a base for them to sit on. Sit them in the buttered muffin tin(s).

Continued overleaf

INGREDIENTS

For the buns:
1 quantity croissant dough
    (see p.66), after the last
    rolling out
butter, at room temperature,
    for greasing

For the filling:
200g light muscovado sugar
100g caster sugar
2 heaped tbsp ground
    cinnamon
120g butter, melted

For the topping:
140g caster sugar
½ tsp ground cinnamon

Makes: 14 buns

The best place to prove the buns is in a completely cold oven. Put them on the centre shelf, along with a small bowl of hot water on the floor of the oven, and shut the door. Leave for 2 hours, until risen and springy to the touch – they won't double in size. Remove from the oven along with the bowl of water. Preheat the oven to 200°C/gas mark 6.

Place the buns in the oven and immediately reduce the temperature to 180°C/gas mark 4. Bake for 25– 30 minutes, until completely puffed and mushroomed over the edges of the muffin cups. They should be a dark, golden brown.

Remove from the oven and leave them for 5 minutes, then lift them and sit them slightly askew in their tins to cool further, so that the base of each bun isn't touching the base of the muffin cup. This allows them to cool without sticking to the cups as the sugar solidifies.

Making the topping by mixing the sugar and cinnamon in a large, shallow dish, and when the buns are completely cooled, roll them gently in the topping to coat them in even more sugary, cinnamony goodness. Eat as soon as possible. If you do have any left over, swap them for the croissants in the Croissant Bake (see p.79), reducing the amount of sugar in the custard by half. You can't even imagine how good this tastes.

TO MAKE IN ADVANCE: If you want fresh buns for breakfast you can put the shaped buns into the fridge overnight, sat in the muffin tins and wrapped in cling film. Just allow them to come to room temperature for 30 minutes or so, then prove and bake as above.

TO FREEZE: Once your buns are shaped, you can cover them in plastic film and freeze in the muffin tins for up to a week. Transfer them to the fridge to defrost overnight, then leave them on the worktop for an hour to come to room temperature, before proving in the oven and baking as above.

RICOTTA, CHERRY AND CRUMBLE CROISSANTS

These are a substantial treat and great to serve for a special breakfast. For this recipe, the older and drier your croissants, the better. You want them to be able to absorb as much new moisture and flavour as possible. The syrup helps the pastry to embrace the ricotta and cherry filling, and when you bake them, it will turn into a delicious gooey pudding. The crumble on top adds a lovely crunch. Buy the best dried sour cherries you can: try to find organic ones – wholefood shops are a good bet.

METHOD

Place the dried sour cherries in a bowl and pour over boiling water to cover, then leave to soak for 30 minutes to grow plump. Drain well.

In a food processor or by hand, mix the icing sugar, softened butter and lemon zest until completely combined. Stir in the egg, then the vanilla seeds. Finally, add the ricotta and the cornflour and mix one last time to give a smooth, creamy texture. Chill, well-covered, for at least an hour or overnight if you prefer. Just before baking, stir in the soaked sour cherries.

Preheat the oven to 170°C/gas mark 3. Use a serrated knife to cut the croissants open along the side of their bellies. Dunk them in syrup and leave a few seconds until thoroughly soaked, then press gently between your palms to drain off any excess syrup. Place the syrup-soaked croissants on a baking sheet lined with non-stick baking paper.

Take a spoon and fill each croissant with the ricotta and cherry mixture through the opening you've made – about 3 generous tablespoons of mixture per croissant. Close them back up and spread another tablespoon of ricotta and cherry mix along their tops, then sprinkle over the crumble and press gently so that it clings to the ricotta.

Bake for 30 minutes, or until the filling is puffed up, cakey, and no longer moist, so you can easily push a knife between it and the croissant. The crumble should be completely crisp, too. Cool for 10 minutes before serving, dusted with icing sugar.

TO MAKE IN ADVANCE: Prepare the croissants right up to the baking stage, then cover with cling film and chill for up to two days. They can go straight from the fridge into the oven, but might need a minute or two longer to bake. Or you can just make the filling a day or two in advance (but don't add the cherries until ready to bake) cover and chill in the fridge.

INGREDIENTS

For the filling:
100g dried sour cherries
80g icing sugar
45g butter, at room
    temperature
½ lemon (finely grated zest)
1 egg
½ vanilla pod, split with
    a knife, seeds scraped
    out and reserved
300g ricotta, drained
1 tbsp cornflour

For the croissants:
6 plain, stale croissants,
    1 or 2 days old
vanilla syrup (p.70)
½ quantity crumble topping
    (p.32)
icing sugar, for dusting

Makes: 6 croissants

CROISSANT BAKE

This is the Cinderella to the not-so-ugly sister that is bread and butter pudding, and another good way to use up leftover croissants. Incredibly rich, it's a very versatile dish – just as good for dessert as it is for a lazy weekend breakfast. If you happen to have a group of friends over this recipe is easy to double up, as we have in the photo.

If you bake Cinnamon Buns (see p.74) and don't manage to eat them all while fresh, you can swap them for the croissants here, reducing the sugar in the custard by half.

METHOD

Use the soft butter to liberally coat the insides of a pudding dish about 20cm x 30cm and 7cm deep. With a sharp, serrated knife, slice the croissants in half. Lay them, cut side down, in the dish with their tails poking up.

To make the custard, beat the eggs in a large bowl. Combine the milk, cream, caster sugar and salt in a medium pan. Use a sharp knife to split open the vanilla pod lengthwise, and scrape out the seeds. Add both pod and seeds to the saucepan. Bring the liquid to the boil over a medium heat, then remove from the heat and pour onto the beaten eggs in a slow stream, just a dribble at first to stop the eggs from from curdling, whisking all the while.

Once all the hot cream has been added, remove the vanilla pod and use a ladle to slowly spoon the custard over the croissants in three batches. The tops of some of the croissants will peak up, Jaws-like, above the custard, so press them down gently. Leave to soak for an hour.

Preheat the oven to 170°C/gas mark 3. Sprinkle the pudding with half the blueberries and bake for 45 minutes, rotating the dish after 25 minutes to ensure an even bake. The finished pudding should be golden brown, springy and moist, but with no liquid custard left. Leave for 10–15 minutes before serving warm, dusted lightly with icing sugar, with the remaining blueberries alongside.

VARIATIONS: Cherries are a great alternative to blueberries – stone them first so your guests aren't left spitting. Or make chocolate-orange pudding by swapping the blueberries for chunks of chopped, dark chocolate. Dollop a few tablespoons of marmalade over the croissants before you ladle over the custard.

TO MAKE IN ADVANCE: The pudding can be left in the fridge overnight to soak in the custard, wrapped in cling film, then go straight into a preheated oven the next day. It might need 5 minutes longer.

INGREDIENTS

For the pudding:
20g butter, at room
    temperature
8 croissants, 1-2 days old

For the custard:
6 eggs
500ml milk
500ml double cream
150g caster sugar
½ tsp fine sea salt
1 vanilla pod
about 300g blueberries
icing sugar, for dusting

Serves: 6

BLUEBERRY MUFFINS

We know how many of our locals love a blueberry muffin with their morning coffee, so here's our take on a recipe that every home baker should have in their repertoire. There's no need to reinvent the wheel when it comes to something as comforting and familiar as a blueberry muffin: we've just added a sprinkling of super-crumbly topping to the classic recipe for even more buttery flavour and contrasting crunch. Proper muffins don't keep well, so genuinely fresh ones – either straight from a bakery, or homemade – will always be preferable. They're simple and quick to bake, but the secret is all in the technique. Sifting the flour gives you a lighter and more aerated result, and the lightness and fluffiness of your muffins depends upon folding the batter together carefully. No need for a mixer here – making muffins by hand is not only quick and easy, but gives better results, and it makes for less washing up to boot. See p.83 for photograph.

METHOD

Preheat the oven to 200°C/gas mark 6. Butter the flat surface of a 12-cup muffin tin thoroughly – that is, all the space between the cups themselves. (The muffins should rise and form mushroom shapes, overflowing slightly onto the top of the muffin tin. Buttering the top of the tin makes it easy to turn them out of the tin after baking.) Line the cups with paper muffin cases. Alternatively, for really tall, shapely muffins, you can do as we do in the bakery and use American popover pans lined with paper cases. These are less easy to find, but make for particularly handsome muffins.

Use a fine sieve to sift together the flour, baking powder, bicarbonate of soda and salt into a large bowl. In a separate bowl, whisk together the eggs and sugar, then the milk, then the melted butter.

Add the egg mixture to the flour mix and fold in gently with a large metal spoon. Avoid over-mixing – better a few lumps than too much stirring, which will result in tough muffins. Set aside a handful of blueberries for topping, then gently stir in the rest.

Divide the batter between the 12 muffin cases and top each with a scattering of crumble, then the remaining blueberries. Place in the oven, then immediately reduce the temperature to 180°C/gas mark 4 and bake for 30–35 minutes, until a skewer inserted into the muffins comes out clean. They should be well-risen, mushroom-shaped and golden.

INGREDIENTS

500g plain flour
1 tsp baking powder
½ tsp bicarbonate of soda
½ tsp fine sea salt
2 eggs
300g caster sugar
350ml milk
120g butter, melted, plus a little extra at room temperature, for greasing
350g fresh blueberries
½ quantity crumble topping (p. 32)

Makes: 12 large muffins

VARIATIONS: This is such a forgiving recipe that you can play around with it in all kinds of ways – use your imagination. Blueberry muffins are our bestsellers but, really, the sky's the limit.

Cinnamon and apple:
A teaspoon of ground cinnamon is a great addition, especially with fresh, diced apples. In fact, you can use almost any fruits, sticking to the proportions given here – even dried ones when seasonal fresh fruits are harder to come by.

Fruit and chocolate:
Try adding a couple of teaspoons of finely grated orange zest along with dark chocolate chips, or using half white chocolate chips and half raspberries (again using the same proportions as the blueberries).

TOASTED BRAN MUFFINS

Bran muffins can be hard to love – they're too virtuous for many tastes, with their whole raisins and their sawdust-like bran. We take those same ingredients but apply a few simple extra steps to transcend them into another universe of flavour and texture. These muffins are brilliant for breakfast, and so filling that eating one in the morning might well see you through till supper (or, at least, lunch) without snacking!

METHOD

Put the currants in a bowl and pour over enough boiling water to cover them. Leave for an hour – or overnight – until they are plump and soft.

Preheat the oven to 150°C/gas mark 2. Butter the flat surface of a 12-cup muffin tin thoroughly – that is, all the space between the cups themselves. (The muffins should rise and form mushroom shapes, overflowing slightly onto the top of the muffin tin. Buttering the top of the tin makes it easy to turn them out of the tin after baking.) Line the cups with paper muffin cases. Alternatively, for really tall, shapely muffins, you can do as we do in the bakery and use American popover pans lined with paper cases. These are less easy to find, but make for particularly handsome muffins.

Spread the bran on a baking sheet lined with non-stick baking paper and toast it in the oven for 15 minutes. The best way to tell whether it's ready is to use your nose – it should smell almost woody. Once your kitchen is filled with its scent, it's ready. The colour will darken slightly, but not too much. Allow to cool completely, and, while it does, increase the oven temperature to 170°C/gas mark 3.

Drain the plump currants and blitz them in a food processor to form a smooth, dark, sticky paste. Put in a large mixing bowl, stir in the toasted bran, along with the sugar, the eggs, orange zest, oil and buttermilk.

Sift together the flour, baking powder, bicarbonate of soda and salt. With a large metal spoon, fold the currant mixture into the dry ingredients until just combined – don't over-mix. Divide the mixture between the 12 muffin cups, and sprinkle over the rolled oats.

Bake for 30–35 minutes. They are ready when well risen, with good, firm tops. These muffins stay incredibly moist, thanks to the currant purée. If you push a skewer into the centre of them, it should emerge with the odd sticky crumb still on it, rather than completely clean.

TO MAKE IN ADVANCE: You can keep the uncooked mixture in a well-covered container in the fridge for a day (or three), taking out as much as you need as and when you want to bake some muffins.

INGREDIENTS

480g currants
190g bran
170g light muscovado sugar
3 eggs
finely grated zest of 1 orange
120ml rapeseed oil
250ml buttermilk
210g plain flour
1 tsp baking powder
1 tsp bicarbonate of soda
½ tsp fine sea salt
a good handful of rolled oats,
    for topping

Makes: 12 large muffins

SOUR CHERRY AND DARK CHOCOLATE DROP SCONES

Just to clarify, we're talking about an American West Coast treat here, and not about the English drop scone, which is a kind of pancake. Our drop scones are more akin to rock cakes in shape, but their texture is completely different.

The trick to getting these right is to use very cold butter, and not to try to mix them into a smooth dough. The lumpier and bumpier, the better. Keep it cold and ugly, and out of the oven will emerge something beautiful and delicious.

METHOD

Sift together the flour, caster sugar, bicarbonate of soda, baking powder and salt in a large mixing bowl. Add the very cold diced butter and use your fingertips to rub it in until the mixture resembles coarse breadcrumbs. You don't need to eliminate every last morsel of butter.

In a small bowl, whisk together the cream and buttermilk. Use your hands to make a well in the centre of the flour mixture, and pour in the liquid in one go. Form one hand into a claw shape and move it gently around in the mixture to stir in the liquids taking care not to leave any untouched patches of dry ingredients. You'll be left with a very sticky, rather ugly dough – don't worry, this is how it's meant to look. Gently add the cherries and chocolate chunks and use your hands to mix them evenly through the dough.

Line a baking sheet with baking paper. Use your hands to scoop 12 tall heaps of dough onto it, without trying to make them too neat – any rough edges will turn wonderfully crispy, crunchy and golden as they bake. Leave at least 5cm between each scone, as they spread out while baking. (Use more than one baking sheet if you need to.) Pop into the freezer for at least 30 minutes.

Preheat the oven to 170°C/gas mark 3. Take the scones out of the freezer, sprinkle lightly with demerara sugar, and bake for 25–30 minutes until their edges are crisp and golden and their insides are still soft. Lift one up gently with a spatula to check that the base is cooked through and has turned an even, dark golden colour.

VARIATIONS: To make blueberry, apricot and ginger drop scones, swap the sour cherries and chocolate for 150g fresh blueberries and 80g dried apricots, 60g crystallised ginger, both chopped small. Make and bake exactly as above.

TO FREEZE: The shaped scones on their baking sheet can be frozen for up to a week. Just take them out of the freezer and bake them in a preheated oven, as and when you want them.

INGREDIENTS

500g plain flour
150g caster sugar
½ tsp bicarbonate of soda
2 tsp baking powder
½ tsp fine sea salt
150g butter, chilled and diced
120ml double cream
175ml buttermilk
150g dried sour cherries,
    roughly chopped
150g dark chocolate, chopped
    into rough chunks
demerara sugar, for sprinkling

Makes: 12 large scones

MAPLE BRIOCHE BUNS

Little *brioche à tête* are a mark of the French breakfast table, but few French people in their right mind would make them when there's always a good neighbourhood *boulangerie* within walking distance. Given that many of us aren't quite so lucky, here's a slightly simpler breakfast bun that's easy to make at home.

METHOD

Take the brioche dough out of the fridge and shape it into 18 little buns (see p.30 for how to shape buns). Place on a baking sheet lined with non-stick baking paper, leaving 5cm gaps between each one. Or, if you'd prefer your finished buns to have a flatter base and a more muffin-like top, you can drop them into the cups of a muffin tin, well-greased with butter.

Put the sheet of buns inside a large plastic bag, well-inflated with air so that the bag doesn't come into contact with the dough, and leave on the worktop to rise again for between 1½ and 2 hours until doubled in size. Preheat the oven to 190°C/gas mark 5.

Brush the tops of the buns with egg wash without applying any pressure – otherwise you'll knock the air out of them. Take a sharp pair of scissors and make two snips in the top of each bun to form a deep cross that cuts almost halfway down through the dough. Sprinkle over a little demerara sugar and bake for 13–15 minutes. They'll open up like tulips as they bake. Test them by lifting one very gently and taking a good look at its base. If it's an even golden brown, your buns are ready.

Take the buns out of the oven and, while still hot, use a pastry brush to coat them with maple syrup. It might seem excessive but use all the syrup. Cool for a few minutes before serving. Our Winter Fruit Compôte (see p.101) is to die for with these or serve with butter, jam, preserves and/ or thick yoghurt.

TO MAKE IN ADVANCE: If you want to bake these fresh for breakfast, leave them to rise overnight in the fridge. Place the baking sheet of buns inside the plastic bag and then put the whole thing into the fridge. They will need an hour out of the fridge to come back to room temperature, plus the 1½– 2 hours rising time.

TO FREEZE: The formed buns can be frozen for up to two weeks. Defrost overnight in the fridge, then leave to come to room temperature for an hour before allowing to rise.

INGREDIENTS

1 quantity brioche dough
    (see p.63), at the end of its
    second rise in the fridge
egg wash (see p.35)
demerara sugar, for sprinkling
130ml maple syrup, clear
honey, or house syrup
    (see p.37)

Makes: 18 small buns

RASPBERRY, RHUBARB AND CUSTARD BRIOCHES

We first came across brioche served as fresh fruit buns at Alice Trent's bakery in Connecticut. It was summer, and she had crushed fresh local raspberries into the buns by hand before baking. We loved the combination of tender brioche dough and tart summer fruit sprinkled with sugar, and when we returned we added these delicious buns to the GAIL's repertoire.

METHOD

To make the brioche buns, take the prepared dough out of the fridge. While it is still cold, use your hands to gently roll it into a sausage shape and cut it into 9 equal pieces. Shape them into little balls by rolling them briefly between the palm of your hand and the worktop. Place these on a baking sheet lined with non-stick baking paper, leaving 5cm gaps between each one. Put the baking sheet inside a large plastic bag, well-inflated with air so that the bag doesn't come into contact with the dough, and leave on the worktop to rise for 1½–2 hours until doubled in size.

While the brioche is rising, toss the rhubarb with the sugar and set aside for 20 minutes until the rhubarb starts to give up its juices. Preheat the oven to 220°C/gas mark 7, and line a baking sheet with non-stick baking paper (for easy cleaning) then stand a wire rack on it. Arrange the rhubarb on the rack in rows, and bake for 12–14 minutes or until the rhubarb is soft, but still holds its shape. Allow to cool. Reduce the oven temperature to 190°C/gas mark 5.

When the brioche buns have risen, remove the plastic bag, take a pastry brush and gently lacquer the buns all over with egg wash. Use two or three fingers to press down gently down into the centre of each bun to create a central well, leaving a generous raised border all around the edge. This will puff up as the buns bake, protecting the filling in the centre.

Drop two generous tablespoons of pastry cream into the well. Top each bun with some rhubarb, sharing the pieces out evenly between the buns, pressing them lightly into the cream. Sprinkle the raw crumble topping around the edge of each brioche and bake for 15–18 minutes until both the dough and the crumble are golden brown. Remove from the oven and leave to cool. Top with the fresh raspberries, and dust with icing sugar before serving.

INGREDIENTS

½ quantity brioche dough (see p.63), after its second rise overnight in the fridge
250g rhubarb, cut in 3cm pieces
50g sugar
egg wash (see p.35)
1 quantity pastry cream (see p.34)
1 quantity crumble topping (see p.32)
1 punnet of raspberries (about 150g)
icing sugar, for dusting

Makes: 9 little buns

VARIATIONS: You can add a spoonful of berry compôte to each
bun before you dust over the icing sugar (see p.100). Or try swapping
blueberries for the raspberries and rhubarb: you'll need 250g fresh
blueberries, pressed gently into the pastry cream on top of each bun
before baking.

TO MAKE IN ADVANCE: The pastry cream must be made a day in
advance, and the rhubarb can be roasted, too. To get much of the work
out the way the day before baking, you can form the brioche buns, place
them on their baking sheet inside a well-inflated plastic bag, and put the
whole thing in the fridge overnight. The next day, take out the fridge, leave
to come to room temperature for an hour, then let rise and bake as above.

TO FREEZE: The formed buns can be frozen for up to two weeks. Defrost
overnight in the fridge, then leave to come to room temperature for an hour
and allow to rise and bake as above.

BRIOCHE PLUM AND GINGER BAKE

We're forever chopping and changing the fresh fruit we use in our kitchen to reflect the passing of the seasons. The English plum season runs from around August through to October, but don't feel you have to restrict yourself to plums. This pudding would work equally well with cherries or peaches. In winter, try using apple, pears or, even, dried fruit, soaked in water or tea.

One important tip: when working with fruit in pastry, choose fruit that is firm, only just ripe, and still very slightly sour. The play on the tongue between the sweet pastry and the added sugar will be enhanced hugely by the tartness of the fruit. Save very ripe fruit for eating on its own, no embellishments needed: it tends to hold too much water to bake with, and will only get mushy in the oven.

METHOD

To make the pudding, use the softened butter to liberally grease a deep pudding dish around 20cm x 28cm. Take the cold brioche dough from the fridge and shape it into 9 equal balls (for how to form balls, see p.30). Place these in the buttered pudding dish, cover with a clean, damp tea towel, and leave on the worktop to rise for 1½–2 hours, until the balls of dough have doubled in size.

Meanwhile, prepare the plums: stone them and cut them into crescent-shaped quarters. Mix them with the demerara and muscovado sugars, the ginger, the water and the lemon juice, and leave to sit for an hour at room temperature, until the fruit starts to give up its juices.

Preheat the oven to 200°C/gas mark 6. Decant the plums and their juice into a roasting tin, and bake for 10–15 minutes. They should be soft, and some should begin to burst and pop, but the wedges should still hold their shape. Leave to cool in the roasting tin.

While the plums cool, make the mixture for soaking the pudding. Heat the milk, butter, caster sugar and ginger in a small saucepan over a low heat, stirring a little, just until the butter has melted. Leave to cool until lukewarm.

INGREDIENTS

For the pudding:
50g butter, at room temperature
½ quantity brioche dough (see p.63), after its second rise overnight in the fridge
10 fresh, just-ripe plums
50g demerara sugar
25g dark muscovado sugar
2 tsp ground ginger
2 tbsp water
½ lemon (juice only)
egg wash (see p.35)
1 quantity crumble topping (see p.32)

To soak the pudding:
50ml milk
50g butter
1 heaped tbsp caster sugar
1 tsp ground ginger

Serves: 6–8

Reduce the oven temperature to 180°C/gas mark 4. Carefully unwrap the risen brioche buns. Use a soft pastry brush to gently brush egg wash over the top of the dough. Pour the lukewarm milky topping all over the pudding, soaking all the dough with the sweet, gingery liquid. Take a sharp pair of scissors and make two snips in each bun to cut a deep cross through them, reaching almost halfway down through the dough.

Take the reserved roasted plums and their juices – don't leave a drop behind, because this stuff is liquid gold – and spoon them evenly between the buns. Scatter the chilled crumble over the top, but don't cover the surface entirely – you want to leave some of the pudding peeking through. Bake for 25–30 minutes until golden brown. Remove from the oven and allow to cool for 10–15 minutes before serving with dollops of thick yoghurt or mascarpone alongside.

TO MAKE IN ADVANCE: The crumble mixture actually benefits from being made a day in advance and left overnight – it just gets all the more crumbly. The brioche buns can also be formed the day before you want to bake the pudding. Shape the buns, sit them in the pudding dish, cover it and chill overnight. The next day, take the dish out the fridge, give the buns an hour to reach room temperature, then leave to rise and bake as above.

BABKA

A funny name, *babka*, and a cake that comes from central Europe, brought to America and Israel. It deserves to be better known here, because it's a beautiful expression of simple home baking.

Gail's grandmother was famous for her delicious babka, which filled the house with an unforgettable smell as they baked – the promise of hot sugar and cinnamon caramelising in the oven, hidden in the folds of a delicious yeast dough. Sometimes there would be hazelnuts, sometimes almonds and raisins. Annoyingly for us, she never wrote down her recipe. The method was 'some of this, and a little bit of that'. When you do something for over 60 years, weights and measures become superfluous. To this day we're still chasing the mirage of that legendary babka, and while we haven't quite got there yet, our version has already created a new generation of fans.

Traditionally, babka wouldn't have used brioche dough, but since we've taught you how to make brioche already, let's keep things simple. In fact, brioche is perfectly good for making babka – perhaps even a little too good!

METHOD

If you can find an angel food cake or any other ring tin around 20cm in diameter, they're perfect for creating the perfect circular crown shape that characterises a babka. But if you can't – and they're not always easily available – you can get clever with a regular round 20cm springform tin. (Prepare the tin for baking by buttering it thoroughly.) Take a small ramekin – about 8cm across and at least 5cm tall – and butter all around its base and outside. Place it in the centre of the cake tin.

When the brioche has risen in the fridge for the second time, make the babka filling. Beat the butter with the dark muscovado sugar until creamy and smooth. You can either do this with a bowl, a wooden spoon, and a little effort, or you can use a stand mixer or hand mixer. Either way, once well combined, add the cinnamon, cocoa powder and salt and mix again briefly before setting aside.

Take the brioche dough and lay it on a lightly floured surface. Dust a rolling pin lightly with flour and roll the dough into a rectangle roughly 40cm x 20cm. Spread the filling evenly all over the dough, except for a 3cm border at one of the longer ends, which should be left free of filling.

Scatter the chocolate across the filling and, starting from the end opposite your 3cm filling-free border, roll the dough up like a Swiss roll, trying to avoid any air pockets from forming as you go. Gently press the dough together to seal up the roll.

Continued overleaf

INGREDIENTS

½ quantity brioche dough (p.63), after its second rise in the fridge
60g butter, at room temperature (plus a little extra for greasing)
90g dark muscovado sugar
1 tsp ground cinnamon
25g cocoa powder
a pinch of fine sea salt
150g dark chocolate, chopped roughly into small chunks
½ quantity of crumble topping (p.32)
egg wash (p.35)

Serves: 6–8

If you or your kitchen are warm, the dough may have become too soft to handle easily by this stage. If so, chill the rolled dough for 30 minutes, covered with a clean, damp tea towel to prevent it from drying out.

When you're ready to continue, take a sharp knife and score down the length of the Swiss roll to create two equal halves. Rotate the halves slightly so that the cut sides are facing towards the ceiling. Lay the halves over each other to form a cross, then form your babka: starting from the centre and working out, one side at a time, scroll the lengths of dough around each other to form a spiral, making sure that the cut, layered sides stay facing upwards at all times. Once you've formed the spiral, carefully lay it in the cake tin, wrapping it around the central funnel (or ramekin if you're using a springform tin). Press the ends together to create a seamless crown of dough.

Cover the tin and its contents with a clean, damp tea towel and leave on the worktop to rise, well away from draughts, until it has doubled in volume – 1½–2 hours.

When nearly ready, preheat the oven to 200°C/gas mark 6. Gently brush the top of the babka with egg wash, then scatter over some crumble here and there, without covering the whole surface of the cake – you want some crunch, yes, but all those beautiful layers should still show through.

Place the babka in the oven and immediately reduce the temperature to 180°C/gas mark 4. After 25 minutes, turn the tin by 180° to ensure an even bake. It will be golden and ready after a total of 40–45 minutes. Let it cool for 15 minutes before even touching it. If you're using a loose-bottomed tin, you can remove it at this point to cool for another 30 minutes. If you're not, leave the babka until just warm before taking it out of its tin. This is so good warm, but shouldn't be eaten straight from the oven – so resist! Put the kettle on and make a cup of coffee while you wait – babka and coffee is a classic pairing. This is best the day it's baked, but you can keep it for 2–3 days in an airtight container. At this stage, once it's a little dry, you might want to experiment with babka toast.

VARIATIONS: To make a cinnamon sugar filling, use a little melted butter to brush the dough, then sprinkle over a generous coating of sugar and a little ground cinnamon – caster or light brown sugar, it's up to you. Chopped walnuts, dried fruits and chopped fresh fruits also make brilliant babka fillings.

MAKE IN ADVANCE: If you want to do the work the day before and have freshly-baked babka in the morning, put the wrapped babka (tin and all) in the fridge before the final rise so that it rises slowly overnight. Come morning, take it out, give it an hour to come to room temperature, and leave it to double in volume before baking.

TO FREEZE: To prepare this well in advance, wrap the shaped babka (tin and all) in cling film before the final rise and freeze it for up to 2 weeks, leaving it in the fridge to thaw overnight the night before you want to bake it. Take it out the fridge, give it an hour to reach room temperature, then let it double in volume before baking.

TOASTED CORNBREAD WITH AVOCADO SALSA AND FRIED EGGS

This Southern-style dish isn't a breakfast for the faint-hearted – it's filling and once you're hooked, you're hooked for life. One important thing to remember about the cornbread is that it benefits from a night or two in the fridge. It somehow matures, so that when you heat it through again, the outsides crisp up beautifully while the insides take on the texture of a delicious, soft pudding. No matter what life's thrown at you, things can't help but look up.

METHOD

Preheat the oven to 170°C/gas mark 3 and butter a baking tin, about 20cm x 30cm. Line it with non-stick baking paper, then butter the paper.

Start by making the cornbread. Whisk together the dry ingredients, then add the grated cheese, the chopped spring onions and chilli. In a separate bowl, whisk together the buttermilk, eggs, olive oil and honey. Combine the wet and dry mixtures to form a fairly thick batter. Pour this into the prepared baking tin and use a spatula to spread it out evenly. Bake for 20–30 minutes, rotating the tin halfway through this time to ensure the cornbread bakes evenly. It's ready when a skewer inserted into the centre comes out clean, the top is golden brown, and it's springy to the touch. Set the cornbread aside to cool completely. If you're making in advance, wrap in cling film and keep in the fridge. Otherwise, go straight on to making the salsa.

To make the salsa – which must be prepared just before serving – peel, stone and roughly chop the avocados. In a bowl, combine with the rest of the ingredients and mix well with a fork. The avocado will break down slightly, but take care to keep the chunky texture. Taste and adjust the seasoning as you see fit, then cover and chill while finishing the dish.

Prepare the lemon oil: warm the olive oil in a small saucepan over a medium-low heat. Add the garlic and crushed coriander seeds. Heat gently to infuse the oil with the flavours for a minute or two, without allowing the garlic or seeds to brown, then set aside. Add the lemon juice and a little salt and pepper to taste, stir again, and leave to cool slightly.

To serve, slice the cornbread into 12 pieces and toast them on both sides. Keep in a warm oven while you fry the eggs in a little butter or oil. Allow two slices of cornbread per person, and drop a large tablespoon of salsa on top of each piece, then a dollop of sour cream. Slide a fried egg or two alongside, and drizzle everything with the warm, fragrant oil.

INGREDIENTS

For the cornbread:
150g plain flour
1 tbsp baking powder
1 tbsp caster sugar
1 tsp fine sea salt
110g fine polenta
70g Gruyère, grated
3-4 spring onions
1 chilli, seeded, and chopped
250ml buttermilk
2 eggs
60ml olive oil
80ml clear honey

For the avocado salsa:
2 ripe avocados
½ lemon (zest and juice)
½ lime (zest and juice)
½ red onion, finely chopped
1 small garlic clove, crushed
1 small chilli, seeded, if liked,
   and finely chopped
½ bunch of coriander leaves
sea salt and freshly ground
   black pepper, to taste
50ml olive oil

For the lemon oil:
30ml olive oil
1 small garlic clove, crushed
1 tsp coriander seeds, crushed
1 lemon (juice only)
sea salt and freshly ground
   black pepper, to taste

To serve:
6-12 eggs
sour cream

Serves: 6

MULTIGRAIN PEAR BIRCHER MUESLI

We're all for an easy life, but you don't need to go out of your way to find the basic ingredients for muesli – they're at any half-decent supermarket. There's no cooking involved, and it's surprisingly good value. You can make as much as you like and change the combination each time – experiment with different grains, add nuts, seeds, dried fruit, fresh fruit – whatever takes your fancy. The whole principle is to use simple, raw, wholesome foods, so bear that in mind. You can use apple juice instead of pear juice, or grated apple instead of pears.

Quinoa flakes (available from wholefood shops) are particularly brilliant here, and freeze-dried berries are delicious, if you can get your hands on them. Begin the day before you want to eat the muesli. See p.98 for photograph.

METHOD

Stir together the oats, barley and rye in a large bowl and pour over the pear juice. Stir again well to mix in. Cover the bowl and leave to soak overnight in the fridge.

At breakfast time, grate the pears and stir into the soaked grains, then crush half the blueberries and spoon into four bowls, swirl through the yoghurt and top with the remaining blueberries.

INGREDIENTS

For the muesli:
60g jumbo rolled oats
60g barley flakes
60g rye flakes
450ml pear juice,
    organic if you can

For the topping:
140g fresh pear
140g Greek yoghurt
100g fresh blueberries

Serves: 4

GRANOLA

Granola is a great breakfast treat and easy to make at home – which also allows you to control exactly what goes into it, and make it rather less sugary than some shop-bought varieties. But it has other uses in the kitchen too, besides breakfast…all the more reason to make plenty of it and store it in a sealed container, where it'll keep for weeks. See p.98–9 for photograph.

METHOD

Put the honey, golden syrup, butter, lemon zest, vanilla, demerara sugar and salt into a saucepan and stir gently over a low heat, until the sugar is completely dissolved. Increase the heat and cook for another 2 minutes to give a glossy, shiny syrup. Set aside to cool a little.

Preheat the oven to 170°C/gas mark 3. In a large bowl, combine all the remaining ingredients except the raisins and sultanas. Pour in the cooled syrup and mix well to coat every speck – you don't want any dry patches left. Line a baking tray with baking paper, and spread the sticky granola evenly across it (use two trays if necessary). Bake for 30 minutes, stirring it every 10 minutes with a wooden spoon to break up the oats into clumps, moving them around slightly to encourage clusters to form. If you like big clusters, be gentle. If you don't, give it a really good stir each time. Once cooked, leave in the baking tin to cool, and don't switch off the oven. If you're a large clusters fan, leave the granola well alone to reach room temperature. If you prefer smaller clusters, continue to stir it occasionally as it cools. Mix in the dried fruit and store in an airtight container. Serve with milk or yoghurt and fruit compôte (see pages 100–1).

INGREDIENTS

180g clear honey
180g golden syrup
180g butter
2 lemons (finely grated zest)
1 tbsp natural vanilla extract
180g demerara sugar
pinch of fine sea salt
450g jumbo rolled oats
100g pumpkin seeds
130g sunflower seeds
200g whole almonds, skins on
200g blanched hazelnuts
1 tbsp ground cinnamon
1 tsp ground nutmeg
½ tsp ground cloves
160g golden raisins (or
    chopped, dried apricots
    or seedless raisins)
130g sultanas

milk or yoghurt and fruit
    compôte, to serve (optional)

Makes: 2kg

THREE FRUIT COMPÔTES

Before international imports made every kind of fruit available all year round, preserving seasonal produce in sugar or alcohol was common practice in every kitchen. These days, most of us go to the supermarket and buy whatever 'fresh' fruit our heart desires, no matter what the time of year. The fruit is often tasteless and hardly fresh, but despite this, we just keep on buying.

If you want to try another way, find out what grows when in the UK and Europe. Make a point of buying at farmers' markets from growers when is the fruit is plentiful and cheap, and turn whatever you can't eat straight away into compôtes to preserve it. They're a doddle to make, and are delicious with yoghurt and cereals, on ice cream or, even, to add a fruity element to a sauce to serve with meat or fish.

Compôte is just a French term that refers to the cooking of fruit in sugar. Together, the sugar, the fruit and the juices it gives off combine to make a delicious syrup. A well-made compôte should enhance the flavour of the fruit, rather than swamping and overpowering it with sugar.

As ever, these recipes are just suggestions. Generally, we like to use fruit that's a little on the tart side and to add as little sugar as possible. If you start with a light dusting of sugar, you can taste and add more as you go along, as and when it's needed.

One final thing: the quantities below are small because they're designed to be used in other recipes. You might want to multiply the recipes by a factor of four or five and make enough compôte to eat up over a few days.

BLUEBERRY AND BLACKCURRANT COMPÔTE

METHOD

Stir all the ingredients together over a low heat in a medium pan until the berries burst and let out their juice, and until the sugar has completely dissolved. Increase the heat and bring to the boil for 2–3 minutes, then reduce the heat and simmer until thick and syrupy – 6–8 minutes. Set aside and cool completely before chilling. This will keep for 2–3 days in the fridge.

INGREDIENTS

200g fresh blueberries
200g fresh blackcurrants
65g caster sugar
1 tbsp lemon juice

Makes: about 450g

PLUM AND RASPBERRY COMPÔTE

METHOD

Stir together all the ingredients except the raspberries in a medium pan over a low heat, until the sugar has completely dissolved. Increase the heat and bring to the boil, then cook for 2–3 minutes. Reduce the heat and simmer until you have a thick sauce – 6–8 minutes. Remove from the heat and stir in the raspberries, but don't let them break down much. Leave to cool completely before chilling. This will keep for 2–3 days in the fridge.

INGREDIENTS

130g plums, stones removed, cut into 6-8 pieces
90g caster sugar
2 tbsp lemon juice
130g fresh raspberries

Makes: about 320g

WINTER FRUIT COMPÔTE

METHOD

Chop the prunes, dried apricots and dried apples into small pieces (if you find they stick to your knife, grease the blade very lightly with oil). Split the vanilla pod with a sharp knife lengthwise and scrape out the seeds, reserving the pod – you will need both it and the seeds.

In a large pan, stir together the sugar, water, lemon juice, lemon rind, spices, vanilla pod and vanilla seeds over a medium heat until all the sugar has dissolved, then increase the heat and bring to the boil. Cook for 2 minutes more, until almost imperceptibly darker – a very pale ivory colour. Add the dried fruits and return to the boil, then reduce the heat and simmer until the mixture is thick, syrupy and the fruits are plump. Leave to cool, pick out and discard the vanilla pod, then chill. This will keep for several months in the fridge.

INGREDIENTS

70g prunes
70g dried apricots
90g dried apples
30g dried cranberries
50g currants
50g sultanas
½ cinnamon stick
1 star anise
½ vanilla pod
½ lemon (pared rind and juice – remove the rind with vegetable peeler)
250g caster sugar
750ml water

Makes: about 750g

MORNING SANDWICHES

Itty bitty little sandwiches like these were inspired by espresso bars in Italy. Italians don't sit down with their morning coffee – they gulp it down and go. And as well as that all-important shot of caffeine, they sometimes grab a simple little sandwich – just some bread and a slice of ham or cheese. It's quick, easy and filling but not overwhelming. You probably don't need to be told how to make a sandwich, but here are two suggestions for fillings which have proved to be big hits with our customers. We like using the Spelt Rolls or Cream Buns (see p.55 or p.56).

PEA AND MINT FRITTATA

METHOD

In a large mixing bowl, lightly whisk the eggs together with the peas, mint, chives, garlic, Parmesan and breadcrumbs. Fold in the ricotta.

Preheat the grill. Heat a dash of olive oil in a large frying pan over a low to medium heat. Very gently pour in the egg mixture and leave to cook for 5 minutes, until you can lift the base with a palette knife and see that it's an even, light golden colour.

Pop the frittata under the grill for 3–5 minutes more, depending on how thick the frittata is – you want it to be completely cooked all the way through so that you can slice it easily for sandwiches.

INGREDIENTS

5 eggs
350g shelled peas – fresh if in season and you have the time to pod them, but otherwise frozen are fine: no need to cook them, just let them thaw for a little
a small handful of fresh mint leaves, roughly chopped
a small bunch of chives, roughly chopped
1 garlic clove, crushed
50g Parmesan, finely grated
50g fresh breadcrumbs, any bread you like
200g ricotta, drained if very wet
olive oil, for frying
rolls, thick yoghurt or labneh and salad leaves, to serve

Makes: 1 frittata (enough for 8 little sandwiches)

SMOKED SALMON AND AVOCADO

Use the best, wild smoked salmon you can find. Slice a ripe avocado thinly and dress it with a little lemon juice to stop it from discolouring. Butter your rolls lightly, fill with a little salmon, a little avocado, and finish with a sprinkling of chopped chives.

BUCKWHEAT PANCAKES WITH CARAMELISED APPLES AND SALTED HONEY BUTTER

Why buckwheat? Well, although these make a brilliant brunch, these aren't your typical American pancakes. They're French-style crêpes, and if you've ever been on holiday to Brittany, the flavour might ring a bell. Buckwheat flour is very popular in that part of France – and for good reason. It's got a much stronger, more distinctive flavour than wheat flour, making these pancakes so much more than just a carrier for the caramelised apples and salty-sweet honey butter.

Buckwheat needs a night soaking in the fridge to give it time to come into its own. That means you'll have to decide the night before that tomorrow morning, you're making pancakes for breakfast. Other than that, these are a doddle to whip up. See p.106 for photograph.

METHOD

Make the pancake batter a day in advance. Sift together the flour and salt. In a separate bowl, whisk together the milk and the egg, then add this to the flour and whisk well until blended and free from lumps. Keep whisking and add the melted butter. Cover the batter with cling film and leave it to rest in the fridge overnight.

These caramelised apples are made without any added sugar – the sugar already present in the fruit is enough. Remove the apple cores and pips – no need to peel – and slice each apple into eight wedges. Heat the butter in a frying pan and, when foaming and hot, tip in the apple wedges and cook until golden brown, turning each wedge over only once. They will need around 5 minutes on each side to caramelise and take on a dark brown colour. Once cooked, set aside and cover with foil to keep warm.

Prepare the salted honey butter: in a small pan over a low heat, warm the honey for a couple of minutes, but don't allow it to boil. Remove from the heat and whisk in the soft butter, one lump at a time, to create a glossy emulsion. Sprinkle in the salt and keep warm until you are ready to serve. If it gets too cool, it will start to solidify, but it can easily be reheated over the gentlest possible heat to liquefy it again.

INGREDIENTS

For the pancakes:
100g wholegrain organic
    buckwheat flour
¼ tsp fine sea salt
1 egg
300ml milk
50g butter, melted
oil or clarified butter,
    for frying

For the caramelised apples:
3 medium Bramley or sour
    Granny Smith apples
30g butter

For the salted honey butter:
80g clear honey
40g butter, at room
    temperature
½ tsp flaked sea salt

4 generous tbsp crème fraîche,
    to serve

Serves: 4

To make the pancakes, decant the batter into a jug to make it easier to pour. Heat a heavy-based frying or sauté pan – or, if you can lay your hands on a special crêpe pan, this is the time to use it – over a medium heat with a little oil or clarified butter. Tilt the pan from side to side to coat the base evenly with oil or butter. If there's any excess, pour it out. When it is good and hot, pour in just enough batter to coat the base of the pan – you want your pancakes to be paper-thin. Swirl the pan to allow the batter to spread over the base. Cook for 2 minutes on the first side until golden. The edges should be so thin that they become crisp and almost lacy. Flip the pancake with a spatula, and cook the second side for a minute or two more. Slide the finished pancake onto a warm plate and keep warm whilst continuing building up a pile of pancakes. Add only the smallest possible amount of oil or butter to the pan and reheat between each pancake.

To serve, take a pancake and fold it in half twice to form a triangle. Give everyone four pancakes, overlapping them the centre of each plate. Arrange six or so apple wedges on top, top with a dollop of crème fraîche, then finish with a drizzle of the warm honey sauce. Don't stint on the sauce here.

BAKED FRENCH TOAST WITH CANDIED BACON

When it comes deciding what to do with leftover bread, there are almost too many choices. Good bread just gets better after a day or two. Its characteristics become more pronounced: it's tangier on the tongue, and chewier, too. The more moisture it loses, the stronger the flavour. At this stage, when it's a little dry, bread is perfect for making French toast. Enriched breads like cholla or brioche are clear winners when it comes to making French toast, but any kind of quality white bread will do.

METHOD

Preheat the oven to 200°C/gas mark 6. To make the candied bacon, spread out the rashers on a wire rack on a baking sheet lined with non-stick baking paper and sprinkle them with the muscovado sugar. Bake for 5–8 minutes, until the sugar has caramelised.

While the bacon is cooking, heat the honey with the cayenne in a small pan, warming it through for a minute until runny. Remove the bacon from the oven and use a pastry brush to lacquer the upper side of the rashers with the honey and cayenne. Return to the oven for 2–3 minutes more. Take them out, turn them over, brush the second sides with honey and cayenne and sprinkle over the finely chopped pecans so that they stick to the honey. Put the bacon back in the oven a final time, and bake until candied and glass-like, another 2–3 minutes – it should take on the shade and the sheen of a glossy conker. Set aside to cool.

To make the French toast, leave the oven on at the same temperature. Whisk together the eggs, milk, cinnamon and salt in a large bowl. Dunk the slices of bread into the liquid and soak until almost falling apart. In a large frying pan, melt a large knob of butter over a medium heat and use it to fry the bread in batches, adding more butter as you go if the pan looks in danger of getting dry. Each side will need 2–3 minutes to turn nicely golden. Flip the bread only once during the cooking process.

When you have fried all the bread, place the slices in a single layer in a large baking tin and bake in the oven for 5–8 minutes, until each slice is a rich golden shade – the edges in particularly should be a dark brown, and the toast should puff up, soufflé-style.

Serve right away: arrange the French toast on plates, top with the candied bacon and drizzle over the maple syrup, honey or house syrup.

INGREDIENTS

For the bacon:
16 rashers rindless unsmoked
    streaky bacon
40g muscovado sugar
2 tbsp clear honey
pinch of cayenne
20g pecans, toasted (see p.35)
    and very finely chopped

For the French toast:
6 eggs
500ml milk
½ tsp ground cinnamon
½ tsp fine sea salt
8 slices (2–3cm thick) of stale
    cholla, brioche or other
    white bread
50g butter, for frying
maple syrup, clear honey,
    or house syrup (p.37),
    for drizzling

Serves: 4

SOFT-BOILED EGGS WITH MARMITE SOLDIERS, FRESH RADISHES AND FROMAGE FRAIS DIP

This is almost more of an idea than a recipe – the individual parts (toast, boiled eggs, a radish salad) are all simple enough, but bringing them all together makes for a brilliant grown-up breakfast combination.

Soft-boiled eggs with their runny yolks are often a question of love or hate. The same, famously, goes for Marmite – so use it in this recipe if you love it, and drop it if you don't. We've also included instructions for making dukkah, an Egyptian spice mix. It's very easy to make, has a million uses, and is utterly delicious. If you for this recipe, you'll have plenty left over, so keep it for months in a sealed jar in a cool, dark cupboard, and sprinkle it on everything from salads to soup. As for the radishes, the French grow what they call breakfast radishes – oblong, pink and white and gorgeous on the plate. They're crisp and fresh, with the faintest, barely perceptible memory of chilli-like heat. Alternatively, if you can find baby radishes, sold in little bags during spring, snap them up. They're punchy little packages of crunch with a peppery kick and are just fabulous in this recipe.

METHOD

First, make the dukkah. Preheat the oven to 180°C/gas mark 4. Scatter the nuts evenly over a baking tray, and the seeds over another (they will cook at different speeds, so this way neither will burn). Roast them until just golden brown, about 5 minutes for the seeds, 10 minutes for the nuts, stirring them once or twice, taking care not to let them burn. Set aside to cool completely, and then blitz the toasted nuts and seeds together in a food processor with all the remaining spices and seasonings. Do this in short bursts using the pulse mode – you want a slightly coarse grind, not a fine powder, so proceed carefully to avoid overdoing it. Once there's no residual heat left in the mixture whatsoever, tip into an airtight jar.

Next, prepare the dip: stir the garlic, salt, pepper and herbs into the fromage frais. Whip the cream by hand using a balloon whisk until it falls in thick folds and holds soft peaks. If you don't mind the extra washing up, you can use a hand mixer – as long as you go carefully and take care not to over-whip. Gently fold the whipped cream through the cheese mix. The texture should be something approaching a mousse. Cover and chill until you need it.

Wash and dry the radishes, discarding any large or damaged leaves. If they're large, slice them lengthwise. Small ones can be left whole.

INGREDIENTS

For the dukkah:
50g blanched almonds
50g hazelnuts
50g walnuts
50g pistachios
35g pumpkin seeds
35g sunflower seeds
35g sesame seeds
2 tsp ground cumin
1 tsp ground cinnamon
pinch of ground cloves
pinch of cayenne
2 tsp fine sea salt
2 tsp freshly ground
    black pepper

For the fromage frais dip:
1 small garlic clove, crushed
½ tsp fine sea salt
¼ tsp white pepper
½ small bunch of chives,
    finely snipped
½ small bunch of dill,
    finely chopped
200g fromage frais
120ml whipping cream

Boil the eggs: cover them with cold water in a saucepan and bring to the boil, then reduce the heat and simmer for 4 minutes. Lift the eggs out of the water and sit them in eggcups. Meanwhile, toast the bread and spread with butter and Marmite (if using). Cut the slices into soldiers.

To serve, arrange each eggcup on a plate, surrounded by Marmite soldiers, and a pile of radishes sprinkled with spring onions and drizzled with olive oil and lemon juice. Drop spoonfuls of fromage frais dip onto each plate and sprinkle a little pile of dukkah next to it.

Dunk the soldiers into the eggs, and the radishes in the dip and the dukkah.

For the radishes:
150g (a small bunch) radishes, green leaves still on if possible
4 spring onions, chopped
sea salt and freshly ground black pepper, to taste
lemon juice and olive oil, to serve

For the eggs and soldiers:
4 eggs
4 slices of sourdough bread butter, for spreading
Marmite, for spreading – optional but always good

Serves: 4

SHAKSHUKA

We think shakshuka is about to take over the world – for a very good reason. It's one of the best breakfasts ever, plus it's incredibly easy to make. This is a communal meal: more than one person can dip into the pan with you, so be sure to share it with someone you love. Making shakshuka is also a perfect opportunity to look through your fridge for any veg that needs using up, and add it to the pan. There are just a few rules to bear in mind. Leave the sauce fairly liquid – that way, it's much easier to mop out of the pan with fresh bread.

METHOD

Heat a large, ovenproof frying pan or sauté pan over a medium heat and toast the caraway seeds for 2 minutes, until very fragrant. Pour in the olive oil and let it warm through, frying the toasted seeds for a minute or two.

Add the sliced onion and pepper and cook, stirring occasionally, until jammy and softened – around 10–15 minutes. Add the chilli flakes, cumin and paprika and cook for a further 2 minutes, until fragrant. Tip in the chopped fresh tomatoes, give everything a good stir, and cook for 5 minutes more until they have completely collapsed and given up their juices. Add the canned tomatoes and bring to the boil. Taste, season with salt and pepper, then cook for 2 minutes more. Reduce the heat and simmer for at least 15–20 minutes, until the sauce is dark, rich and flavoursome. If it becomes too thick, you can always thin it with a little water. If necessary, you can remove from the heat and leave the sauce to cool down until you are ready to serve, at which point simply heat it up and carry on to the next stage.

Preheat the oven to 200°C/gas mark 6. Take a wooden spoon and hollow out a little well in the surface of the tomato sauce. Gently break an egg into it, taking care not to break the yolk. Continue to plant the eggs around the pan until you've added them all. Take a fork and bury the egg whites under the sauce while leaving the yolks on show.

Crumble the feta over the top in between the yolks, drizzle the top with olive oil to prevent it from burning and give it a lovely shine, and place the pan in the oven. After 5 minutes, the yolks should be just set. After 5 minutes, the yolks should be set – bake them for less if you'd like them runny. Sprinkle over the chopped coriander leaves and drizzle with olive oil to serve. Put the pan directly on the table along with the best white sourdough you can find, sliced or, even, toasted, if you like. The traditional, communal way to eat shakshuka is straight out of the pan, scooping it up with pieces of bread, but plates are allowed if you really insist.

VARIATIONS: This sauce is so versatile – it's amazing served with baked fish, for example. To make it meatier, add grilled merguez sausages or slices of cooked chorizo.

INGREDIENTS

½ tsp caraway seeds
50ml olive oil
1 onion, thinly sliced
1 red pepper, seeded
    and thinly sliced
½ tsp dried chilli flakes
½ tsp ground cumin
½ tsp smoked, hot or
    sweet paprika, to taste
3 tomatoes, chopped
2 x 400g cans chopped tomatoes
8 eggs
50g feta
extra virgin olive oil,
    for drizzling
a handful of coriander leaves,
    chopped
sea salt and freshly ground
    black pepper, to taste
1 whole good, white sourdough
    loaf, sliced, to serve

Serves: 4

BRIOCHE AND HOMEMADE SAUSAGE TARTS

These sausage tarts are the savoury sisters of our Raspberry, Rhubarb and Custard Brioches (see p.88), and the method of forming and filling them is exactly the same. Making your own sausage mix takes no time, but it's the best way to ensure you have it just the way you like it, and avoids the nasties that lurk in some shop-bought sausages.

METHOD

Make the sausagemeat first. Break the bread into fine crumbs by hand or in a food processor. In a large mixing bowl, add the breadcrumbs to the minced pork along with all the other ingredients and mix well by hand. Chill, covered, for at least an hour or overnight.

Take the brioche dough out of the fridge, and, on a lightly floured surface, shape it into 9 buns (see p.30 for how to shape buns). Place these on a baking sheet lined with non-stick baking paper, leaving 5cm gaps. Put the baking sheet inside a large plastic bag, well-inflated with air so that the bag doesn't come into contact with the dough, and leave on the worktop to rise for 1½–2 hours until doubled in size. While the buns are rising, make the crème fraîche filling by stirring together all the ingredients. Chill for at least an hour.

When the brioche are risen, take a pastry brush and gently lacquer the buns all over with egg wash. Use your fingers to press down down into the centre of each bun to create a central well, leaving a generous raised border all around the edge.

Preheat the oven to 190°C/gas mark 5. Drop a generous tablespoon of crème fraîche mixture into the centre of each brioche, then divide the pork mixture into 9 parts. Shape and flatten each patty so that it sits comfortably in the centre of the brioche, on top of the crème fraîche. Drizzle each bun with a little melted butter and season. Bake for 15–20 minutes, until the brioches are golden and the sausage cooked through.

Serve warm from the oven with a green salad dressed with olive oil, and wedges of hard-boiled eggs.

TO MAKE IN ADVANCE: Both the sausagemeat and crème fraîche filling can be made a day in advance. You can also form the brioche buns, place them on their baking sheet inside a well-inflated plastic bag, and put the whole thing in the fridge overnight. The next day, take it out of the fridge, leave to come to room temperature for an hour, then let rise and bake as above.

INGREDIENTS

For the homemade
    sausagemeat:
300g minced pork
1 large slice of stale sourdough
    bread, crusts removed
1 tsp dried oregano
a very good grinding
    of black pepper
1 tbsp wholegrain mustard
5 sprigs of thyme, leaves only,
    finely chopped
2 sprigs of rosemary, leaves
    only, finely chopped
5 fresh sage leaves, finely
    chopped
1 egg, beaten

For the tarts:
½ quantity brioche dough
    (see p.63), after its second
    rise in the fridge
egg wash (p.35)
40g butter, melted
flaked sea salt and freshly
    ground black pepper, to taste

For the crème fraîche filling:
180ml crème fraîche
75g wholegrain mustard
60g Parmesan, finely grated
½ small bunch of chives,
    finely snipped

Makes: 9 small tarts

EGGS IN THE NEST WITH WILTED GREENS

We don't suppose for a moment that anybody's childhood memories of their parents trying to entice them to eat a wholesome breakfast are as good as this. Still, it's our memories of that old favourite, 'eggs in the nest', that inspired us to come up with this recipe – giving it a grown-up twist in the process. After all, there's no good reason to forget something as delicious as eggs in the nest just because we're a bit older now…

Store the egg whites in the fridge and use for meringues or an egg white omelette: whip them until stiff, season and add some chopped fresh herbs. Fry on one side then flash under a hot grill to brown and puff up.

METHOD

In a large pan (one with a lid), heat a knob of butter and little olive oil over a medium heat. Add the onion and cook, stirring, for about 5 minutes until soft, then add the crushed garlic and cook for a further 2 minutes, not allowing it to brown. Tip in all the greens, reduce the heat, give them a stir and then cover to allow them to steam until they collapse to barely a third of their original volume – the water left clinging to the leaves after washing them helps the greens to cook.

Uncover the pan, pour in the double cream and increase the heat to bring the liquid to the boil. Let it bubble away until the cream has reduced and thickened, then season with Parmesan, salt, white pepper and nutmeg. Remove from the heat and squeeze in the lemon juice.

Meanwhile preheat the oven to 200°C/gas mark 6. If you have pastry cutters, use one to cut a circle from the centre of each slice of bread. If you don't, use the rim of a glass about 5cm in diameter. Heat a frying pan with a knob of butter and a splash of olive oil, and fry the slices of bread on both sides until golden.

Line a baking sheet with non-stick baking paper, and lay the slices of fried bread on it. Spoon the wilted, creamy greens into the nest at the centre of each slice, then use a teaspoon to make a small well in each mound of greens. Drop an egg yolk into each well. Slide the baking sheet into the oven and bake for 8–12 minutes, depending on how runny you like your yolks.

VARIATIONS: Sliced smoked salmon isn't strictly necessary, but makes a brilliant addition served alongside – and perhaps a green salad too. Duck egg yolks are amazing here for added richness and flavour.

TO MAKE IN ADVANCE: The wilted greens can be made a day in advance, cooled quickly and kept, covered, in the fridge until you need them.

INGREDIENTS

For the eggs in the nest:
4 slices of sourdough bread, about 2cm thick
4 egg yolks
olive oil and butter, for frying

For the wilted greens:
1 onion, finely chopped
1 garlic clove, crushed
80g baby spinach, washed and drained, but not dried
80g chard (Swiss, baby or rainbow are all good here), tough stalks removed, leaves washed and drained, but not dried
80g rocket
1 large bunch of fresh basil
80g watercress
120ml double cream
60g Parmesan, finely grated
flaked salt, ground white pepper and grated nutmeg, to taste
a squeeze of lemon juice
butter and olive oil, for frying

Makes: 4

CROQUE MADAME

The classic croque monsieur is so much more than a simple cheese and ham toasted sandwich with a fancy French name. A croque madame takes this superstar sandwich to the next level by topping it off with a softly cooked egg.

METHOD

It's best to make the sauce up to a day in advance to give it time to chill and set. Melt the butter in small saucepan and add the flour. Cook, stirring continuously with a wooden spoon, for 3–4 minutes until golden brown and giving off a nutty scent. Switch to a hand whisk and add the milk very gradually in stages (to avoid lumps), whisking well all the time. Once all the milk is added and the sauce is smooth, increase the heat to bring it to the boil, but don't stop whisking. Season with salt, pepper, nutmeg and cayenne, then remove from the heat and add the grated cheese and mustard. Stir until the cheese has melted and the sauce is completely smooth. Decant into a container and cover with cling film, pressing it right down to touch the whole surface of the sauce – this prevents a skin from forming. Cool then chill until needed.

Preheat the oven to 200°C/gas mark 6. Cover four slices of bread with a generous layer of béchamel sauce, reserving plenty for topping. Lay a slice of ham over the sauce, followed by a good covering of half the grated Gruyère. Top with the remaining slices of bread, then coat the top and sides of each sandwich with the remaining sauce. Imagine you're icing a cake, but instead of icing, you've got béchamel, and instead of a cake, you've got a sandwich. Finish with a sprinkling of Gruyère.

Using a fish slice, carefully transfer the sandwiches to a baking sheet and bake for 10–12 minutes. The cheese should turn a dark, burnished gold as it melts, and the base of each sandwich will caramelise. The cheese inside should be molten – test it by pushing a knife into the sandwich, then touching the knife quickly on the back of your hand. If it feels hot, then the sandwiches are cooked through. Transfer to warm serving plates.

While the sandwiches are baking, fry the eggs in a hot frying pan with a little butter. Slide a fried egg onto each sandwich and season with salt and pepper to taste before serving. If you want to serve these with anything, a simply dressed green salad is all they need.

VARIATIONS: Try swapping the ham for flakes of smoked mackerel and thinly sliced leeks cooked in butter until soft. Or replace the ham and Gruyère with slices of soppressata or other salami or a smear of nduja or other spreading sausage and goat's cheese. Black pudding is also to die for here.

INGREDIENTS

For the cheesy béchamel sauce:
40g butter
40g plain flour
250ml milk
¼ tsp fine sea salt
¼ tsp ground white pepper
a pinch of grated nutmeg
a pinch of cayenne
100g strong Cheddar, grated
1 tsp Dijon mustard

For the sandwiches:
8 thick slices of cholla, brioche or other good, soft white bread
4 slices of ham, large enough to cover the bread (honey-glazed if possible)
100g Gruyère, grated
4 eggs
butter, for frying

a dressed green salad, to serve

Makes: 4

LUNCH

SEEDED BUTTERMILK CRACKERS

You might not think crackers are much to get excited about – so why would you make them at home? But these are a different beast entirely – these are the crackers that ate London and that London can't stop eating. Deeply savoury and fragrant with seeds, they're so moreish that they should carry a health warning, and so simple to make that it's all too easy to feed your addiction.

METHOD

To make the crackers, sift together the flour, sugar, baking power and salt into a large bowl. Scatter over the cubes of cold butter and use your fingertips to rub them gently into the dry ingredients until you have something resembling breadcrumbs.

Pour in the buttermilk, mixing with a wooden spoon as you go, until you're left with a smooth dough. Wrap in cling film and chill overnight.

The next day, preheat your oven to 200°C/gas mark 6 and take the dough out of the fridge. Line two baking sheets with baking parchment. Lightly flour your work surface, divide the dough in half and use a rolling pin to roll each piece into a rectangle, as thin as you can while still fitting onto the baking sheets. Work fast, keeping the dough as cold as possible. If it gets too warm, chill in the fridge again before continuing. Wrap each rectangle of dough around your floured rolling pin and unravel it carefully onto a baking sheet.

To make the topping, mix the salt with the seeds and sprinkle it liberally all over the dough, pressing in the seeds gently with your palms.

Bake for around 15 minutes (rotating the baking sheets 180° halfway through to ensure they cook evenly) until they are a light golden colour all over. Leave to cool, then use your hands to break into jagged shards. Serve with dips or plain, at a casual spread or with a glass of Champagne. These are as versatile as crackers come.

INGREDIENTS

For the crackers:
400g plain flour, plus extra
   for dusting
20g caster sugar
½ tsp baking powder
½ tsp fine sea salt
100g butter, chilled and diced
250ml buttermilk

For the topping:
1 tsp flaked sea salt
1 tsp each of sesame, caraway,
nigella, poppy and fennel
seeds and golden linseeds

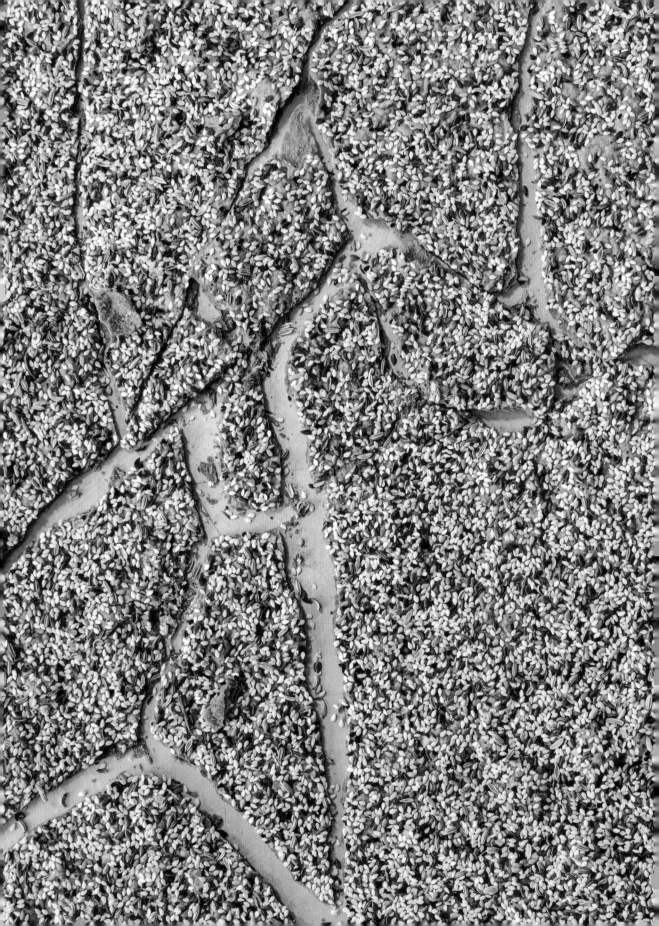

SAVOURY BISCOTTI

Sometimes mistakes can lead to breakthroughs. We had, originally, set out to create something not far from a giant savoury loaf-like scone, or a richly flavoured soda bread, but it just wasn't working. We made it flatter and, although it baked better, it still didn't taste of much. Discouraged, we went home for the night.

The next morning, Gerry Moss (bless his soul) decided to cut our abandoned loaf into thin slices and toast them in the oven. Suddenly we found ourselves with something incredibly delicious – crisp, savoury and moreish. Whether the flavours needed that extra time to come together, or it was the way the loaf had dried out overnight, we couldn't say – but something magic happened.

'Biscotti' means twice-baked, so while you might not want to dunk one of these in your coffee, it's an accurate description nonetheless. They are delicious served with soups, cheese, charcuterie or salads.

METHOD

First, roast the sweet potato. Preheat the oven to 180°C/gas mark 4. Wash the sweet potato, dry it well, wrap it tightly in foil and roast for 30–45 minutes until you can push a sharp knife all the way into it with no resistance. Unwrap it carefully and leave until cool enough to handle, then cut in half. Scoop the flesh into a mixing bowl and mash roughly with a fork, then set aside.

Meanwhile, roast the chorizo in a small baking dish for 5 minutes until cooked through – when ready, it will begin to ooze its bright orange oil, and shrink a little. Set aside, but leave the oven on.

To make the biscotti, mix together the flour, baking power and bicarbonate of soda. To the bowl containing the sweet potato, add the grated onion, the rosemary, the feta, the cooked chorizo and the olives. Give the mixture a good stir with a fork until everything is combined. Sprinkle the flour mixture over the sweet potato mixture and toss with your hands so that everything is coated with the flour.

In a separate bowl, whisk the egg into the buttermilk along with the mustard. Pour the egg mixture onto the sweet potato mix and stir to combine into a rough, loose dough, but don't overwork it.

Continued overleaf

INGREDIENTS

1 sweet potato (190g
    peeled weight)
75g cooking chorizo,
    cut into thin slices
190g plain flour, plus extra
    for dusting
1 tsp baking powder
1 tsp bicarbonate of soda
1 red onion, grated
3 sprigs of rosemary, leaves
    only, roughly chopped
100g feta, crumbled
75g stoned Kalamata olives
1 large egg
3 tbsp buttermilk
2 tsp Dijon mustard

Makes: about 20 biscotti

Dust a baking sheet with flour and pour the sticky mixture onto it. With floured hands, shape into a flat round of dough, about 7–8cm high. Dust the top with a very sparing amount of extra flour, and bake for 1¼ hours until cooked right through. Leave to cool for 5–10 minutes, then transfer to a wire rack and leave to cool completely.

Finally, slice your cooked dough into the 'biscotti'. With a sharp, serrated knife, cut the loaf into 1cm-thick slices. Lay these evenly on a baking sheet, and put back into the oven until toasty and very crisp, but not totally dried out.

VARIATIONS: Other kinds of sausage or cooked bacon are equally good in place of the chorizo, or you can leave out the meat altogether to cater for vegetarians. The sweet potato can be swapped for butternut squash or just potato, and the cheese can be varied too. Just keep the proportions the same, and you're free to experiment with the flavours as much as you like.

TO MAKE IN ADVANCE: After the first round in the oven, the whole loaf can be wrapped in cling film and kept in the fridge for a couple of days before slicing and baking for the second time.

CHEESE STRAWS

This recipe won't turn out cheese straws exactly like those you'll find in our bakeries or in most shops because in this recipe we use flaky fromage frais pastry, which is much quicker to make. They're a slightly homier version – a bit plumper, a bit less dainty, and just as packed with flavour, but a little less fiddly to make.

These are the perfect snack with pre-dinner drinks – they're intensely savoury, and can be made as mild or as spicy as you want. Mix up the herbs, or leave them out entirely – go minimalist, or go wild.

METHOD

Preheat your oven to 200°C/gas mark 6 and line a baking sheet with non-stick baking paper.

Roll out the chilled pastry on a lightly floured surface with a floured rolling pin to give a rough 30cm x 25cm rectangle: it doesn't have to be perfect or neat.

With the short edges of the rectangle to your left and right, spread the mustard thinly all over the surface using the back of a spoon. Season the dough well with salt, pepper and cayenne – how much depends on how much spice you like.

Scatter the cheese over the half of the dough closest to you, then top with the sliced onion and sprinkle with the basil. Fold the top half of the dough down over the bottom half to cover it completely, then press it down all over to seal in the filling. (If at any point the pastry becomes too soft to handle easily, transfer everything to the fridge for 20 minutes to firm up.)

Cut the rectangle in half from top to bottom, then cut each half into 6 strips, giving 12 in total, each about 12cm long. Once cut, brush them all with egg wash. Hold each strip at both ends and twist two or three times to form spirals. Lay them on the lined baking sheet and bake for 18–20 minutes until the cheese is dark golden and the straws are completely crisp all the way through – you don't want any sogginess. Leave to cool slightly then serve. These are best eaten right away, but are still good the day after: 5 minutes in a hot oven will restore them almost to their former glory.

INGREDIENTS

1 quantity flaky fromage frais pastry (see p.33)
1 tbsp Dijon mustard
sea salt, freshly ground black pepper and cayenne, to taste
120g strong cheese, grated – we like to use Gruyère but any strong, hard cheese will do, such as a mature Cheddar
½ small red onion, thinly sliced
5 sprigs of basil, leaves only, roughly chopped
egg wash (see p.35)
flour, for dusting

Makes: 12 chunky cheese straws

HAM AND CHEESE CROISSANTS

Half the pleasure of this recipe lies in the fact that almost everything can be done well in advance. The other half is that they're so very, very good!

At GAIL's, we usually assemble our ham and cheese croissants in the afternoon, then store them overnight in the fridge. Come morning, they go directly into a very hot oven until the heat penetrates right to their cores and melts the cheese within, giving them the oozing, molten centres that we love.

METHOD

Preheat the oven to 190°C/gas mark 5. With a sharp, serrated knife, slice the croissants open lengthwise down one side to form pockets.

Spread the insides evenly with some of the béchamel sauce and lay a slice of ham across the bottom half. Sprinkle over a handful of Gruyère (reserving some for topping) and close them up.

Spread a little more béchamel on top of each croissant, and finish with another sprinkling of Gruyère. Bake until the cheese is golden brown and the croissant itself is crisp and flaky – around 10–15 minutes. Eat while still warm if you possibly can.

VARIATION: For a veggie option, sauté a small garlic clove and 120g sliced leek in 30g butter for 8–10 minutes, stirring occasionally. Add 200g roughly chopped mushrooms, 1 tbsp olive oil and 2 tsp fresh thyme leaves and cook, stirring until soft, and the moisture has evaporated. Use in place of the slice of ham in each croissant.

INGREDIENTS

6 plain croissants,
    at least a day old
1 quantity cheesy béchamel
    sauce (see p.119)
6 slices of ham
180g Gruyère, grated

Makes: 6 croissants

SAUSAGE ROLLS

We think these are the best sausage rolls on the planet, and few who try them disagree. They're a bit fatter than the ones you're likely to be familiar with – we used to make ours thinner, but when you've gone to the trouble of making your own sausagemeat and it's as delicious as this, why wouldn't you want to pack more into each one?

METHOD

Preheat the oven to 200°C/gas mark 6 and line a baking sheet with non-stick baking paper.

Roll out the pastry on a lightly floured surface to give a rectangle measuring 30cm x 40cm. Lay it in front of you so that the short sides are to your left and right. Cut it in half horizontally with a sharp knife, so that you have two 15cm x 40cm rectangles. (If at any point in the process the dough becomes too soft to handle, just put everything in the fridge for 20 minutes to firm up again.)

Cut the sausagemeat in half. Shape each into a log the length of the pastry rectangles. Place one along the centre of one of the rectangles. Brush the top edge of the rectangle with egg wash, then fold up the bottom edge to cover the sausage, but not so that it meets the top edge. Roll the rectangle away from you so that the pastry wraps around itself slightly, sealing up along the egg-washed edge. Repeat with the second rectangle and the second sausagemeat roll.

Cut each giant sausage roll into 7 equal pieces to give you 14 in total. Egg-wash their tops and sprinkle with a mixture of the seeds. Lay them on the baking sheet, well spaced out, and bake for 25–30 minutes, until the sausage is cooked right through and the pastry is dark golden and crisp. Serve as they should be – with ketchup.

INGREDIENTS

1 quantity flaky fromage
   frais pastry, well chilled
   (see p.33)
2 x quantities of sausagemeat
   (see p.116)
egg wash (see p.35)
2 tsp sesame seeds
2 tsp nigella seeds
GAIL's ketchup, to serve
   (see p.37)
flour, for dusting

Makes: 14 rolls

CARAMELISED ONION AND VINTAGE CHEDDAR BRIOCHE BUNS

We make these savoury brioche buns with all kinds of fillings in the bakery, depending on the time of year. They're ideal for lunch on the go as an alternative to a sandwich. This particular version is inspired by pissaladière, a classic pizza-like Provençale dish of caramelised onions baked atop bread dough. While it's full of flavours from the sunny south, the ingredients work well in winter, too.

METHOD

Melt the butter with the olive oil in a large frying pan over a medium heat. Add the onions and cook until softened, stirring from time to time – about 10 minutes.

Add the thyme, demerara sugar, balsamic vinegar and salt. Cook for another 15–20 minutes, stirring occasionally, until the onion has caramelised and turned dark golden. The mixture should be sticky, but not dry. Turn everything into a colander to drain off any excess oil and juices. Leave to cool to room temperature, then fish out the sprigs of thyme and discard.

While the filling cools, roll out the very cold brioche dough on a lightly floured surface, forming a rectangle, roughly 30cm by 40cm. Lay the rectangle in front of you so its short edges are to your left and right. Spread the onions over the dough, leaving a 4cm border along the long, top edge, then sprinkle the Cheddar over evenly. Roll the dough up from the bottom towards the top like a Swiss roll. Cut in half to give two shorter roulades, then slice each half into 6 buns.

Butter a 12-cup muffin tin generously, then sit the buns in the cups, so that one of their swirled, cut ends faces upwards. Pop inside a large plastic bag, inflated so that the bag won't come into contact with the dough, and leave at room temperature to rise for 1½–2 hours – the brioches will puff up, but won't double in size. Preheat the oven to 180°C/gas mark 4.

Remove the dough from the plastic bag. Brush the top of each bun lightly with egg wash and bake for 20–30 minutes, until the dough is a dark golden brown. Carefully lift up one bun and check that its base is cooked right through – it should be much darker than the tops.

Take out of the oven and leave to cool for 5–10 minutes on a wire rack, then turn out of their tins and eat while the cheese is still gooey.

VARIATIONS: Take the Provençale touch even further by laying a few anchovies over the onion filling, or mixing in some roughly chopped olives.

INGREDIENTS

20g butter, plus a little
    extra for greasing
4 tbsp olive oil
4 large onions, thinly sliced
5 sprigs of thyme
2 tbsp demerara sugar
2 tbsp balsamic vinegar
½ tsp fine sea salt
120g coarsely grated
    vintage Cheddar
1 quantity brioche dough
    (see p.63), after its rise
    overnight in the fridge
egg wash (see p.35)
flour, for dusting

Makes: 12 buns

GRUYÈRE AND CHIVE SCONES

We started making these scones in GAIL's Kitchen during winter, when we put a gorgeously rich, creamy seafood chowder on the menu. We'd thought about topping it with a savoury cobbler or perhaps little cheese dumplings, but it was too good-looking to cover up. These little scones were designed to be served alongside. They were so delicious they even outshone the chowder itself – good as it was – so we now make them as a stand-alone recipe.

METHOD

Preheat the oven to 180°C/gas mark 4 and line a baking sheet with non-stick baking paper. Sift the flour, baking powder and salt together in a large bowl, then tip in the cold cubes of butter. With your fingertips, rub the butter into the flour until the mixture resembles coarse breadcrumbs, but try to leave a few little nuggets of butter scattered through it. Use your hands to mix in the cheese and the chives.

In a separate bowl, whisk the eggs and milk together, then form a well in the centre of the flour mixture. Pour in the milk and eggs all in one go, stirring gently with a wooden spoon as you go. The finished mixture will be sticky and very lumpy. Think scrambled eggs, and you're not far off.

Use your hands to form the scones: wet your palms slightly to prevent the dough from sticking to them and scoop it up in handfuls, dropping it in 12 mounds onto the lined baking sheet. Leave 5cm gaps between each one to allow for spreading, and don't worry about forming perfect shapes – any cragginess or rough edges will just give you even more flavour and texture. Bake for 20–25 minutes until golden brown and crisp on the outside, but still soft inside. These make a brilliant alternative to bread with all kinds of soups, stews or casseroles. Or you can split them, fill them, and serve them like mini-sandwiches.

VARIATIONS: Any strong hard cheese will work, as will plenty of other herbs – thyme, for example.

TO FREEZE: Open-freeze the shaped scones on the baking sheet then wrap and freeze for up to a week. Just take them out as and when you want to bake them – an easy route to freshly-baked scones every day with almost no extra effort.

INGREDIENTS

360g plain flour
2 tsp baking powder
1 tsp fine sea salt
170g butter, chilled and diced
250g Gruyère, grated
small bunch of chives,
    finely snipped
4 eggs
150ml milk

Makes: 12 scones

CHEESE, SPINACH AND TOMATO SCONE TRAY

Here's another way to inject scone dough with intense, savoury flavours – a filling of cheese, greens and ripe tomatoes. Serve while still warm as a light meal or as a friend for your Sunday roast.

METHOD

Preheat the oven to 170°C/gas mark 3 and line a baking dish roughly 25cm x 35cm and 4cm deep with non-stick baking paper. Grease the paper with a little olive oil.

To make the dough, sift together the flour, baking powder, salt and cayenne in a large bowl, and add the chilled cubes of butter. Rub the butter into the flour with your fingertips until the mixture resembles breadcrumbs. Stir in the grated cheeses.

In a separate bowl, whisk together the egg and the milk, then add this to the flour mix and stir lightly with a spoon until just combined – don't over-mix. The mixture will be more like a batter – incredibly wet and lumpy – and you might worry that nothing good will come of it, but trust that it will, and resist the temptation to make a smooth dough.

Stir together all the ingredients for the filling except the oil, vinegar and seasoning in a large mixing bowl, tossing them together as if you were making a salad. Add a few drops of vinegar and a little olive oil at first, then more if you think they're needed. Season, to taste.

Take half the dough and scoop lumps of it into the tray. With the back of a large spoon, dipped in water so it doesn't stick to the dough, press the lumps down into a reasonably even layer that covers the whole of the base of the tray. Pour the filling evenly over the dough, including all the juice. Scoop the rest of the dough on top, moving it around with the wet spoon to cover all the filling. Top with the slices of tomatoes, some black pepper and flaked sea salt, and a drizzle of olive oil. Bake the giant scone for 25–30 minutes, rotating it half way through the baking time to ensure an even bake. Test it by sliding a palette knife or spatula under the bottom and lifting it up to peek at the base. If it's an even, golden brown, the scone is cooked all the way through. As soon as you take it out of the oven, scatter over the grated Parmesan. Serve warm. This won't cut into neat slices, so don't bother to try.

VARIATIONS: In winter, cubes of roasted root vegetables would be perfect in the filling. Almost any hard cheese is great, and slices of Parma ham, fried lardons or pancetta should appease keen carnivores.

INGREDIENTS

For the dough:
500g plain flour
2 tbsp baking powder
½ tsp fine sea salt
¼ tsp cayenne
75g butter, chilled and diced
125g Cheddar, grated
50g Parmesan, grated
1 egg, beaten
400ml milk

For the filling:
100g Cheddar, grated
40g Parmesan, grated
50g goat's cheese, crumbled
½ red onion, thinly sliced
60g baby spinach
a small bunch of basil,
    leaves only
10 cherry tomatoes, halved
1 tbsp red wine vinegar
2 tbsp olive oil
salt and freshly ground black
    pepper, to taste
dried chilli flakes, to taste
¼ tsp freshly grated nutmeg,
    or to taste

For the topping:
2 tomatoes, cut into thin slices
a good grinding of black pepper
flaked sea salt, for sprinkling
olive oil, for drizzling
50g Parmesan, finely grated

Serves: 10–12

SMOKED SALMON AND SPINACH TART

A bit of a controversial ingredient, smoked salmon. We love it, but were keen only to use it at GAIL's if it was sustainable, top-quality fish. Good environmentally friendly wild salmon doesn't come cheap, though, so it's something of an occasional treat. It's so delicious that if you do invest in some for a special occasion, this tart is a clever way to make it go a lot further. On another note, for the gluten free brigade, the filling can be cooked in a baking tray lined with non-stick baking paper to make a smoked salmon crustless tart.

METHOD

Make the dressing by whisking together all the ingredients. Set to one side.

Heat the olive oil in a pan over a medium heat. Fry the onions until translucent, stirring regularly – about 6–8 minutes – then add the crushed garlic. Cook for 2–3 minutes until the garlic is fragrant, but not coloured.

Add the spring onions and cook for 2 minutes until softened, then add the spinach (still damp from rinsing) and the rocket. Let them wilt and collapse in the pan before adding the dill and the cream. Simmer for 5 minutes until the mixture reduces and thickens slightly, then taste and season with white pepper, salt, nutmeg and mustard. Pour into a clean bowl and leave to cool, then chill. When the mixture is cold, mix the beaten eggs into the greens and set aside.

Meanwhile, lightly dust the worktop and rolling pin with flour and roll out the pastry to a rectangle roughly 30cm x 40cm. Use the pastry to line a baking dish about 25cm x 35cm, and 4 cm deep. To transfer the pastry sheet easily to the dish, roll it around onto your rolling pin, position it at the end of the baking dish and unroll the dough into the dish. Press the pastry into the base up the sides to form a rough tart case, then chill for an hour in the fridge or 30 minutes in the freezer.

Preheat the oven to 180°C/gas mark 4 and put a baking sheet in the oven to heat up. Lay and fold the slices of smoked salmon in the chilled pastry case so that they don't sit flat. Imagine slicing the tart, and make sure that everyone will get a fair portion of fish. Pour the prepared filling into the case, so that the folds of smoked salmon are still peaking above the liquid.

Place on the hot baking sheet and bake for 35–40 minutes until the base is golden brown. Leave to cool slightly, slice, and serve warm with the honey and mustard dressing drizzled over and a salad on the side.

VARIATIONS: Smoked salmon has a very strong flavour when baked, so if you want something slightly milder, try flakes of hot-smoked salmon. Smoked trout or mackerel are also good alternatives.

INGREDIENTS

For the honey and mustard dressing:
50g Dijon mustard
50g clear honey
5 sprigs of dill, finely chopped

For the tart:
3 tbsp olive oil
400g onions, sliced
1 small garlic clove, crushed
1 bunch of spring onions, chopped
200g baby spinach, washed and drained, but not dried
1 large bunch of rocket
1 small bunch of dill, roughly chopped
200ml double cream
½ tsp white pepper
½ tsp fine sea salt
¼ tsp freshly grated nutmeg
½ tsp Dijon mustard
3 eggs, beaten
1 quantity flaky fromage frais pastry (see p.33)
flour, for dusting
300g smoked salmon

Serves: 10

FRESH HERB TART

Like a garden baked into a tart. Imagine the soft, delicate textures, flavours and colours of an English summer herb garden, suspended in a pale, creamy custard and held in a crisp pastry case. This exceptionally beautiful tart works with all kinds of herbs (but avoid strong, dominant flavours such as coriander or rosemary). Don't chop the herbs too finely, and don't over-mix or let them break up too much. This recipe makes enough pastry for two. The other half can be kept in the fridge for three days, or frozen for a week and defrosted overnight in the fridge.

METHOD

First, make the pastry. In the bowl of a stand mixer fitted with the beater attachment, beat the butter until smooth and soft. Stop the machine, scrape it down, and add the cornflour, egg yolk, water, salt and sugar. Mix again on low speed until a soft paste forms. Stop, scrape and add the flour, then mix slowly until you have a soft dough. Flatten out into a thick disc and wrap in cling film. Chill for at least 2 hours, or overnight.

Cut the pastry in half and roll one half out on a lightly floured surface to 3mm thick disc. Use it to line a 24cm tart tin and bake blind (p.31). Set the baked case aside to cool completely. Reduce the oven temperature to 180°C/gas mark 4.

To make the filling, melt the butter in a frying pan and cook the onion, spring onions and garlic over a medium heat until very soft – about 10 minutes. Set aside to cool slightly.

Whisk together the eggs, crème fraîche, double cream, salt, pepper and ground coriander. Add the cooled onion mixture to this custard and mix well. Stir in all the herbs, coating them well, then mix in the grated cheese. Pour the herb custard into the tart case and bake for 10 minutes, or until very slightly coloured. Reduce the temperature to 170°C/gas mark 3 and bake for a further 20–25 minutes. Try to keep this tart beautifully light in colour, so the colours of all the herbs shine through the pale custard. Remove from the oven as soon as it's completely set. Serve while still warm, perhaps with an extra dollop of crème fraîche.

INGREDIENTS

For the pastry:
120g butter, at room
    temperature
60g cornflour
1 egg yolk
2 tbsp water
½ tsp fine sea salt
1 tsp caster sugar
130g plain flour

For the filling:
25g butter
1 onion, thinly sliced
4 spring onions, finely chopped
3 garlic cloves, finely sliced
3 eggs
100ml crème fraîche, plus
    extra to serve (optional)
120ml double cream
¼ tsp salt
¼ tsp freshly ground
    black pepper
¼ tsp coriander seeds,
    lighted toasted and
    ground to a powder
120g mature Cheddar, grated
2 sprigs of parsley, leaves only,
    roughly chopped
4 sprigs each of tarragon,
    thyme, oregano, marjoram,
    and chervil, leaves only,
    roughly chopped
2 tbsp snipped chives

Serves: 8

BACON AND EGG TART

Bacon and eggs: a classic British combo, but it took the Kiwis to turn them into such a lovely, rustic pie. This is the GAIL's take on a typical New Zealand recipe that sees a shortcrust tart case filled with eggs and bacon. We've swapped that shortcrust for our soft, slightly sweet cream bun dough, and added a rich savoury custard, both of which work brilliantly with the intensely savoury bacon. The key to this recipe is its simplicity: resist the temptation to add more flavours to the filling.

This is crying out to be served with a green salad – crisp and sharp with a mustard, lemon or garlic dressing.

METHOD

Line a rectangular baking tray or shallow baking dish with non-stick baking paper. On a lightly floured surface, roll out the cream bun dough so that it's large enough to line a 25cm x 30cm baking tray with the rim. Carefully lift the dough into the tray, and push it out evenly with your fingertips. If you find the dough resists and won't let you push it around, give it 5 minutes to rest, then try again. Put inside a large plastic bag, inflated so that it won't come into contact with the dough, and leave to rise at room temperature for 1½–2 hours until doubled in size.

Meanwhile, preheat the oven to 200°C/gas mark 6. Line a baking tray with non-stick baking paper and arrange the rashers of bacon on it. Roast for 5 minutes until just cooked, then set aside to cool and reduce the oven temperature to 180°C/gas mark 4. While the bacon cools, make the filling by whisking together all the ingredients except the cheese in a large jug.

Remove the risen dough from the bag and flatten it with your fingertips so that it can hold the bacon easily, leaving a raised lip around the edge. It should be dimpled – not dissimilar to a focaccia. Lay the rashers evenly across the surface of the dough. Break the eggs directly onto it, inbetween the rashers. Imagine cutting it into slices and try to make sure that every slice will include both egg and bacon. Pour on the filling, trickling it all around the eggs and bacon to encourage it to spread evenly. Finish with a generous scattering of grated Cheddar and bake for 45 minutes, until the custard has set and the tart is a dark, fragrant, golden brown.

Serve warm or cold, cut in slices. (When cold, wrapped well, it makes the best packed lunch.)

VARIATIONS: If you don't want to make a yeasted dough, swap the cream bun base for flaky fromage frais pastry (see p.33), any good shortcrust pastry, or even good quality shop-bought all-butter puff pastry.

INGREDIENTS

For the tart:
½ quantity cream bun dough, after its first rise in the bowl (see p.56)
10 rashers (about 450g) of rindless back bacon, smoked or unsmoked
10 eggs

For the filling:
250ml double cream
180ml crème fraîche
2 egg yolks
½ tsp fine sea salt
½ tsp white pepper
¼ tsp grated nutmeg
½ tsp Dijon mustard
150g grated Cheddar
flour, for dusting

Serves: 10

PUY LENTIL, ROASTED BEETROOT AND GOAT'S CHEESE SALAD

This is Emma's favourite salad and she's not alone. It's a lunchtime staple in the bakeries: filling, but not too heavy. This recipe gives you a good opportunity to play with the huge variety of beetroot available. Use as many kinds as you can get your hands on, especially in spring and summer when heritage varieties are available in all their rainbow array.

The dressing is particularly unusual and really helps this salad stand out. It makes use of the fantastically savoury flavour of sun-dried tomatoes – not sunblushed tomatoes, which are softer, and not the kind stored in oil. The ones you want for this recipe are the moreishly salty ones sold, dried and rather hardened, in little bags. (See p.144 bottom-left, for photograph.)

METHOD

Preheat the oven to 180°C/gas mark 4. Rub the beetroot skins with the 2 tablespoons olive oil (or more if you need it), wrap them tightly in foil, sit them in a baking tin and roast for an hour, or until completely soft when tested with a sharp knife. The cooking time will very much depend on the size of the beetroot. Leave to cool for 10–15 minutes then unwrap, and use a knife to strip off the skin. Slice into wedges so you can see all the nice layers of colour inside the root – if they're small, or particularly pretty, you could just cut them into cross-sections to expose the ringed layers. Set aside.

Meanwhile, cook the lentils in plenty of unsalted, boiling water until just tender, but still *al dente* – about 15 minutes. Add the teaspoon of salt to the water, simmer for a minute more, then drain and rinse the lentils under cold water. Set aside.

Make the dressing: soak the sun-dried tomatoes in hot water for 10 minutes to rehydrate them. Drain, then squeeze out the excess water. Put everything except the rapeseed oil in a blender or food processor and blitz to make a relatively smooth paste. With the motor still running, gradually add the rapeseed oil, until you have a thick dressing.

In a large mixing bowl, combine the cooked lentils, the rocket and the dressing, and toss lightly until just coated.

Pile the dressed lentils on a flat serving platter, then the beetroot, then crumble the goat's cheese over and, finally, the chopped hazelnuts. Drizzle over a final ribbon of olive oil, and set on the table for everyone to dig in.

INGREDIENTS

400g raw beetroot
2 tbsp olive oil, plus extra
    for drizzling
240g Puy lentils
1 tsp fine sea salt

For the dressing:
40g sun-dried tomatoes
1 tbsp wholegrain mustard
1 garlic clove, crushed
2 tbsp red wine vinegar
a good grinding of
    black pepper
8 sprigs of mint, leaves only
1 tbsp clear honey
50ml olive oil
50ml rapeseed oil, or other
    neutral flavoured oil

To finish:
40g rocket
120g soft, fresh goat's cheese
40g blanched hazelnuts,
    toasted and very roughly
    chopped

Serves: 4

BLACK BARLEY AND SMOKED SALMON SALAD

Black barley is a fascinating but unusual ingredient. The little black pearls are wonderfully chewy, and completely different in both flavour and texture from the rice, quinoa or couscous that you'll often find in similar salads. If you can't track it down, you could swap in farro, pearl barley, or wheat berries.

Invest in your smoked salmon: buy the best, sustainably sourced fish you can afford. You don't need much of it, and it will make all the difference. This recipe will leave you with plenty of dressing left over, but it keeps well in the fridge to use with other salads. (See p.145 for photograph.)

METHOD

Begin by making the dressing: mix together the mustard, pepper, salt, lemon juice and vinegar, either in a food processor, with a hand-held blender, or with a balloon whisk. Continue to mix as you add the olive oil all in one go, then trickle in the rapeseed oil in a fine ribbon to form an emulsion.

Make the salad: cook the black barley in unsalted water according to the packet directions. When ready, its texture will be chewy and slightly resistant as you bite into it, but with no crunch or hard core. A minute before it's done, add the salt to the cooking water. Drain, rinse it under cold water, drain again then toss with a splash of olive oil.

Toss together all the remaining salad ingredients, except the smoked salmon, with 160ml of the dressing. Serve in one large bowl, or divide up into serving dishes, with the slices of salmon folded on top.

VARIATIONS: Swap the cucumbers for roasted courgette or diced avocado. Either chop 400g courgettes into 2cm cubes, toss with a little olive oil, salt and pepper, and roast at 220°C/gas mark 7 for 10 minutes until slightly golden but not too soft. Leave to cool, then mix into the salad. For avocado, use half a fruit per person. Simply peel, dice, and toss them in a little lemon juice to prevent browning then add to the salad.

INGREDIENTS

For the mustard dressing:
40g Dijon mustard
½ tsp ground black pepper
2 tsp fine sea salt
1 lemon (juice only)
3 tbsp white wine vinegar
150ml olive oil plus extra
    for garnish
200ml rapeseed oil (or other
    neutral flavoured oil)

For the salad:
200g black barley
1 tsp fine sea salt
1 large or 2–3 small cucumbers
    (about 400g), seeded if
    large, and diced
6 sprigs of dill, finely chopped
6 spring onions, finely chopped
50g mixed leaves (rocket, baby
    chard, baby spinach etc.)
200g smoked salmon

Serves: 4

LEMON CHICKEN, OLIVE AND FREGOLA SALAD

This isn't a dieter's salad – it makes for a filling, hearty meal. Fregola looks like a grain at first glance, but it's actually, a traditionally Sardinian toasted pasta made from semolina, and this salad is packed with the flavours of the Mediterranean. You'll have more aioli than you need for this salad, but it keeps well in a sealed container in the fridge for a few days, so save what's left and use it as a dip for crudités, in sandwiches or just spread on toast – we're addicted! (See p.144, top-left, for photograph.)

METHOD

First, make the aioli. Preheat the oven to 180°C/gas mark 4, rub the bulbs of garlic in oil and then wrap in foil. Roast for an hour, until each bulb is soft and collapsing when pierced with a knife. Leave to cool until you can handle safely, then unwrap the foil and squish each bulb well with a fork to press all the soft, roasted flesh out of the papery skins. Discard everything but this golden purée, then mash and chop it further if necessary until you're left with a really smooth paste. Stir the garlic purée into the mayonnaise along with the lemon juice, then set aside. Increase the oven temperature to 220°C/gas mark 7.

Next, make the lemon chicken. In a large mixing bowl, combine the chicken thighs, thyme, olive oil, salt, pepper, crushed garlic and olives. Take the lemon slices and squeeze them over the chicken, wringing out all the juice so that all you're left with are the finely sliced skins, then mix these in too.

Spread the mixture out in a baking dish, tucking the olives underneath the other ingredients – they tend to burn otherwise. Cook for 15–20 minutes until the chicken is completely cooked through and the lemon is just beginning to brown. Allow to cool, then roughly chop into bite-sized pieces.

Meanwhile, cook the fregola in boiling, salted water according to the packet directions, then drain, rinse under cold water, drain again and toss with a little olive oil to prevent it from sticking together.

Blanch the French beans in boiling, salted water for 8 minutes until tender – you don't want them too crisp for this recipe – then drain, rinse under cold water and drain again.

To assemble, mix half the aioli with the fregola, watercress, beans, chicken mixture, and some extra olive oil – plus salt and pepper if you think it needs it – and serve at room temperature.

INGREDIENTS

For the roasted garlic aioli:
130g mayonnaise (homemade, see p.36, or a top quality brand)
2 whole garlic bulbs
2–3 tbsp olive oil
½ large lemon (juice only)

For the lemon chicken:
400g free-range skinless, boneless chicken thighs (or ask the butcher to skin and bone them for you)
5 sprigs of thyme, leaves only
20ml olive oil
½ tsp flaked sea salt
a good grinding of black pepper
2 garlic cloves, crushed
80 g stoned Kalamata olives
1 large unwaxed lemon, cut in half lengthwise, then into the thinnest possible, virtually transparent slices, all pips discarded

For the salad:
250g fregola
150g fine French beans, topped and tailed
40g or 1 small bunch of watercress
olive oil, salt and pepper, for dressing

Serves: 4

RED QUINOA SALAD WITH SMOKY AUBERGINE YOGHURT

The smoky aubergine topping on this salad has become something of a breakout star in its own right. It's won so many fans that we now sell it on its own, to use as a dip, a sauce for lightly cooked vegetables, or a topping for crackers. Given that, it might be worth doubling up the quantities given here and keeping it in the fridge for all kinds of uses. Here, it provides a creamy contrast to the zingy, crunchy, wholesome salad underneath.

You can use dried chickpeas in this recipe, as we do in the bakery – soaking them overnight, changing the water twice, then boiling them for an hour until softened. But, given that such a small quantity is required here, we've listed canned chickpeas in the ingredients. If you want to use dried chickpeas, you'll need 50g. (See p.145, top-right, for photograph.)

METHOD

Begin by making the smoky aubergine yoghurt. Preheat your oven to 220°C/gas mark 7. With a sharp knife, cross-hatch the flesh of the aubergines on their cut sides, then sprinkle with salt and olive oil. Bake, cut sides up, for 20–30 minutes until soft and yielding when tested with a knife. Leave to cool until you can handle them easily, then scoop out all the flesh with a spoon and discard the skins. Chop and mash the flesh to a smooth pulp, then mix in all the other ingredients, tasting to check the seasoning. Cover and chill until needed.

Meanwhile, make the salad: cook the quinoa according to the packet directions, then drain and rinse under cold water shaking off all the excess water. Toss together all the ingredients until everything is well coated with lemon juice and olive oil. Spoon into bowls and serve with a good dollop of the aubergine yoghurt on top, so everyone can stir it in as they eat.

INGREDIENTS

For the smoky aubergine
    yoghurt:
2 medium aubergines,
    halved lengthwise
fine sea salt and olive oil,
    for sprinkling and seasoning
1 garlic clove, crushed
50g tahini paste
120g very thick Greek yoghurt
½ lemon (juice only)

For the salad:
80g red quinoa
80g canned chickpeas, drained
80g fresh or frozen peas,
    blanched
1 large or 3 small cucumbers,
    seeded and diced into
    1.5cm dice
3 spring onions, roughly
    chopped
handful each of fresh coriander
    and parsley, leaves only,
    roughly chopped
1 lemon (zest and juice)
1 red pepper, seeded and
    cut into 1.5cm dice
2–3 tbsp olive oil
1 tsp salt
1 tsp freshly ground
    black pepper
80g baby spinach, washed
    and drained

Serves: 4

TUNA NIÇOISE ON TOAST

In the bakeries we now sell a version of this recipe as a sandwich – in a baguette, bien sûr – but the inspiration came out of GAIL's Kitchen, where it started life as a very superior kind of tuna and egg sourdough bruschetta. We take the classic ingredients of a Niçoise salad, with all those summer, south-of-France flavours, and cook them together in a stew that makes an excellent topping for toast.

METHOD

Begin by making the stew: warm the olive oil in a large pan. Add the chilli flakes, herbs, onion, olives and capers. Stir well and cook over a medium heat for 8–10 minutes, until the onion is soft and everything is permeated with the fragrance of the herbs. Add the garlic and cook for 1 minute more, stirring the whole time. Slowly add the tomatoes, and, depending on how juicy they are, an extra splash of water. You're looking to create a thick stew, and some liquids will continue to evaporate off, so use your judgement. Bring to the boil, season with the salt and pepper, then add the French beans and the potatoes. Reduce the heat and simmer until the beans are very soft, and the potatoes are cooked through. Remove from the heat, add the lemon juice, sprinkle over the parsley and leave to cool for 30 minutes.

Soft-boil the eggs for 5 minutes in a pan of simmering water. You want them softer than a properly hard-boiled egg, but not quite as runny as you'd leave them for serving with soldiers. (We often cook one extra egg, just in case something goes wrong, which is why this recipe calls for five and not four eggs.) Immediately fish out of the pan, tap lightly with a spoon to crack the shells slightly, and put into a bowl of cold water. Leave to cool, then gently peel.

Brush the sourdough all over with olive oil and toast on both sides under a hot grill.

Divide the toast between 4 plates and pile the stew on top, then add large flakes of tuna without breaking them up. Place the eggs on top, breaking them in half with a spoon so the yolks begins to run out. Lay over the anchovies, sprinkle with the chopped parsley, and drizzle with a little more olive oil. Serve while still warm.

INGREDIENTS

For the stew:
3 tbsp olive oil
½ tsp dried chilli flakes
10 sprigs of thyme, leaves only
2 sprigs of rosemary, leaves only
1 onion, chopped
20g stoned black olives
1 tbsp capers in brine, drained
2 garlic cloves, crushed
400g can chopped tomatoes
1 tsp fine sea salt
½ tsp freshly ground
    black pepper
50g French beans,
    topped and tailed
80g bite-sized new potatoes,
    well-scrubbed (if you
    can only find larger ones,
    just halve them)
½ lemon (juice only)
small bunch of parsley,
    roughly chopped

To finish:
5 eggs, at room temperature
4 thick slices of sourdough
    bread
olive oil, for brushing and
    drizzling
200g tuna fillets in olive oil,
    drained – pick a Spanish
    brand if you can
12 anchovy fillets, preserved
    in oil – the best you can get
small handful of fresh parsley,
    leaves only, roughly chopped

Makes: 4

BAKED BREAD AND CHICKEN SOUP

When we first opened GAIL's Kitchen, it was November, and we were fast heading towards the dark days of winter. We were looking for a recipe that would encapsulate everything we wanted to do at the restaurant – to build great meals around bread – and that would see us through those cold months. We found it in this soup.

It's a country-style soup: nothing too refined or delicate, just strong, rustic flavours, drawing on the very strong tradition of bread soups found in Italian cooking – think of ribollita, or pappa pomodoro. They all make use of the wholesome, comforting qualities of bread. We also love the fact that we can bake this in the oven – which, as bakers, is at the centre of everything we do.

METHOD

Pour the chicken stock into a large saucepan and bring it to the boil over a medium heat. Season with a little flaked sea salt, then lower the chicken breasts into the hot liquid. Return to the boil, then reduce the heat and simmer for 5 minutes. Remove the pan from the heat and leave it to stand for 1 hour. Lift out the chicken breasts with a slotted spoon and set aside, reserving the stock. When the chicken is cool enough to handle, use a couple of forks to shred it into chunks, rather like pulled pork.

Preheat your oven to 200°C/gas mark 6. Warm the olive oil in a large, deep frying pan over a medium heat. Once hot, add the pancetta and cook, stirring occasionally, for 5 minutes. Stir in the diced onions and cook for 10–12 minutes until very soft, stirring from time to time. Add the garlic and the cabbage, give everything a good stir for a minute or two, then add the shredded chicken and pour in the reserved stock. Bring to the boil, then reduce the heat and simmer until the cabbage is tender – about 15 minutes. Taste and season with a little extra salt or some pepper, if necessary.

Ladle half the hot soup into six ovenproof bowls or little casseroles, filling each just less than half-way, and making sure that everyone gets their fair share of cabbage, pancetta and chicken. Fit a slice of bread on top of each bowl (trimming, as necessary, to fit), and scatter over half the grated cheese. Top up the bowls with the remaining soup, lay another slice of bread over it, and finish with the remaining cheese. Press down on the cheesy top layer of bread to soak it thoroughly in the broth, then place the bowls on baking trays, transfer carefully to the oven, and bake until the cheese is golden brown and bubbling – 8–10 minutes.

INGREDIENTS

2 litres chicken stock (homemade or top-quality shop-bought)
2 chicken breasts, on the bone, skin on
2 tbsp olive oil
100g pancetta, in 1cm cubes
2 small onions, diced
3 garlic cloves, chopped
500g Savoy cabbage, sliced into fettucini-like ribbons
12 slices of sourdough bread, crust left on, about 1cm thick
150g vintage Cheddar or Gruyére, grated – pick a cheese strong enough to sting your mouth
flaked sea salt, to taste
freshly ground black pepper, to taste

Serves: 6

WELSH RAREBIT WITH SMOKED MACKEREL

Welsh rarebit is the savoury to end all savouries: a great British classic. Our version will tick all your boxes if, like us, you love smoked mackerel. Buy the best-quality fish you can find – you don't want synthetic smoke flavouring to dominate the delicate mix. Look for good, fatty fish that falls into large flakes when cooked.

If you don't use all the topping at once, it will keep well in an airtight container in the fridge for up to 3 days. Whenever the mood takes you, toast a piece of bread, spread it over and grill until gold and bubbling for almost instant rarebit satisfaction.

METHOD

Sit the mackerel snugly in a small pan, pour over the milk, and bring gently to the boil. Once it has boiled, remove from the heat, put the lid on the pan, and leave to infuse for 10–15 minutes. Lift the fish out of the milk, keeping the liquid to hand. Remove the skin from the fillet and discard. Flake the fish into bite-sized pieces and set aside to cool.

In a second, small pan, melt the butter. Once melted and just foaming, sprinkle over the flour, stirring well with a wooden spoon to form a smooth paste. Cook for two minutes or so until golden, stirring all the while, then gradually pour in the milk you used to cook the fish. Don't stop stirring! Add the Guinness next, and stir until the sauce has thickened. Remove from the heat and stir in the cheese, mustard and Worcestershire sauce, until the cheese has completely melted and the sauce is smooth. Finish by stirring in half the chopped parsley leaves.

Fold the flaked fish into the sauce. At this stage, you can either leave to this to cool, chill it overnight, and use it the next day, or you can carry straight on to make the rarebit now. Toast the slices of bread lightly, then slather each slice generously and reasonably evenly with the rarebit topping. Pop under a hot grill until the fish and cheese bubble and darken. A few black spots here and there are no bad thing. Sprinkle with the remaining parsley to serve, perhaps with a crisp side salad.

INGREDIENTS

250g smoked mackerel fillet, bones removed
150ml milk
30g butter
30g plain flour
80ml Guinness, or other stout
50g mature Cheddar, grated
1 tsp wholegrain mustard
1 tsp Worcestershire sauce
a handful of fresh flat leaf parsley, leaves only, finely chopped
flaked sea salt and freshly ground black pepper, to taste
6 slices of your favourite bread – we love to make this with sourdough
crisp mixed salad, to serve

Makes: 6

TRUFFLE, RACLETTE AND SHALLOT TOASTIE

You don't always need to make everything from scratch. Some things are best left to the experts, and that's definitely the case with truffle butter. It's not an everyday item, and it's almost impossible to make on your own. Go to the pros, take pleasure in what they've made, and do something with it. While truffle butter may not be cheap, you only need to use a smear at a time to turn this dish into something really special.

This is a real cold-weather dish – think of the earthy scent of a wood in winter, then of skiing and the classic warming melted cheese dishes that are almost all you want to eat when you're on the slopes. And yet, despite its luxurious ingredients, it's still just a toastie – something you really ought to eat with your hands.

METHOD

Slice the shallots in half lengthwise, without peeling them. Take a pan big enough for all the halved shallots to sit on the bottom, and melt the knob of butter over a medium-low heat. Nestle the shallots, cut side down, on the base, then cover with a sheet of non-stick baking paper. Sit a plate on top to weigh everything down, and leave for 6 minutes to caramelise. The butter will begin to burn very slightly, and the shallots will soften. If they're not quite soft all the way through after 6 minutes, heat the oven to 180°C/gas mark 4 and roast them for 5–10 minutes until they are. When ready, sprinkle their cut sides with a few drops of sherry vinegar to cut through the richness, and sprinkle with sea salt. Leave to cool, then peel away the layers, stripping them back one at a time to leave soft, golden, translucent leaves of shallot.

Spread the slices of bread on one side with a thin smear of truffle butter. Lay the slices of raclette onto four pieces of bread, then top with the leaves of softened shallot. Close up with the remaining slices of bread. If you have a toastie maker, use that to toast the sandwiches on a low heat. If not, use a lightly-greased griddle pan: put the toasties in it, cover with non-stick baking paper, sit a plate on top to weigh them down, and cook gently on both sides, turning once, until the cheese is melting and golden.

These are even better when served with a little glass of something to cut through the richness – kirsch, perhaps, or even schnapps. Dry sherry would also go down very well.

INGREDIENTS

4 large banana shallots
a knob of butter, for frying
a few drops of sherry vinegar
flaked sea salt, to taste
8 slices of sourdough bread –
    the more holey, the better
    (our San Francisco
    sourdough is perfect for
    this: the super-slow
    fermentation creates large
    holes through each loaf)
4 tsp truffle butter
200g raclette cheese, sliced

Makes: 4

MEATBALL SANDWICHES

The meatball sandwich must be one of the greatest and most excessive expressions of the art of American sandwich making. A good meatball sandwich is humongous, delicious, and absolutely merits the effort of cooking your own meatballs. If you don't like pork, you can use all beef or lamb. The quantities here can easily be doubled or even tripled – you could make more than you need, and serve the rest with pasta.

METHOD

First, make the meatballs. Soak the bread in the milk until it's absorbed, then squeeze it to remove any excess liquid (there may not be any, depending on how dry your bread was to begin with). Tip the soggy bread into a large bowl and add all the other meatball ingredients apart from the flour. Mix together well with your hands to combine thoroughly, but don't overwork. Go gently and use your fingers lightly: don't squish or pummel. Use your hands to shape the mixture into 12 meatballs. Line a baking sheet with non-stick baking paper and sit them on it. Cover with cling film, and chill for at least an hour.

To make the sauce, heat the olive oil in a large pan. Fry the sliced garlic briefly for about a minute, taking care not to let it colour. Add the tomato purée and cook for a couple of minutes, until it becomes darker and richer in colour. Add the tomatoes and water and bring to the boil, then reduce the heat and simmer for 30 minutes. Season to taste with salt and pepper. Remove from the heat and add the whole basil leaves.

Preheat the oven to 200°C/gas mark 6. Dust the meatballs in a very light coating of plain flour, shaking the baking sheet to ensure they're completely covered. Bake for 8–10 minutes to sear them on their outsides – they don't need to cook through, just take on a nice colour. While the meatballs are baking, take a large, deep baking dish – about 20cm x 28cm and 7cm deep is ideal – and pour in the sauce. Take the meatballs out of the oven and reduce the temperature to 180°C/gas mark 4. Float the seared meatballs in the sauce, leaving their tops bobbing above the surface, then return the whole thing to the oven for an hour.

Either serve immediately, or, for an even tastier sandwich, cool, then reheat thoroughly in the oven the next day before serving. Excellent between two slices of sourdough, or crammed into a cream bun, not forgetting a generous sprinkling of grated Parmesan, Gruyère or Comté to top them off. Cook in the oven or under the grill to melt the cheese.

INGREDIENTS

For the meatballs:
30g (about one slice) stale
    white sourdough bread
1½ tbsp milk
½ small red onion, finely diced
small bunch of flat leaf parsley,
    leaves only, finely chopped
250g minced beef
250g minced pork
60g Parmesan, finely grated
1 sprig of rosemary, leaves
    only, finely chopped
3 sprigs of thyme, leaves only,
    finely chopped
2 garlic cloves, crushed
1 tsp fine sea salt
1 tsp freshly ground black pepper
1 egg
a little plain flour, for dusting

For the sauce:
3 tbsp olive oil
1 garlic clove, thinly sliced
2 tbsp tomato purée
2 x 400g cans chopped tomatoes
250ml water
1 bunch of basil, leaves only
salt and freshly ground
    black pepper, to taste

To serve:
8 slices of sourdough bread, rolls
    or Cream Buns (see p. 56)
grated cheese (optional)

Makes: 4

BARBECUE PULLED PORK SANDWICHES WITH PICKLED CUCUMBERS

As far as we're concerned, almost everything tastes better between two pieces of bread. These are seriously juicy sandwiches, full of delicious hot barbecue sauce. Don't wear white while eating them – they're just too messy. Think of a big party, and imagine something fantastic to serve with cold beer and good music that's easy to put together at the last minute – these are just the ticket. By the time you're in the swing of things, you'll have forgotten that it's taken you two days to prepare the pork…

This makes enough pulled pork to fill at least 12 sandwiches and probably more, but it's difficult to make in smaller quantities, and too time-consuming for that to be worthwhile. Because of that it's great for a large gathering, but if there aren't a lot of you, you can either eat it up throughout the week, or freeze some for later, or use it in another recipe (see the variations below).

If you want to simplify the recipe, feel free to leave out the barbecue sauce. The pork will still be delicious as it is.

METHOD

Begin two days before you want to serve the sandwiches. First, make the pork rub by mixing all the ingredients except the pork together. Use your hands to massage the rub into the meat, getting the flavours into every nook and cranny. Wrap the pork shoulder very tightly in cling film to seal it, then put it in the fridge overnight, where it will take on all the flavours of the rub.

The next day, preheat the oven to 150°C/gas mark 2. Remove the pork from the fridge, and pour 500ml water into a roasting tin large enough to hold the meat. Sit the pork in it, and wrap the whole tray tightly in foil, twice – this will trap in the steam and protect the meat from burning. Roast for 5½ hours.

Meanwhile make the pickled cucumbers. Bring all the ingredients except the sliced cucumber and onion to the boil in a small pan. Arrange the cucumber and onion in a dish and pour over the hot pickling juice. Leave to cool, then cover and chill.

When the pork is cooked, remove it from the oven, it should be tender and falling apart. Take care when removing the foil, as the hot steam will escape. Allow it to cool a little until you can handle it easily. Remove the top layer of fat and discard, then use two forks to shred the meat into strings. Fish the shredded meat out of the braising liquid and put into a clean bowl. Pour the braising liquid into a pot or dish and chill it until the fat rises to the surface and solidifies. Scoop this off and discard: you'll be left with a small amount of incredibly flavoursome liquid.

INGREDIENTS

For the pork:
5 garlic cloves, crushed
100g wholegrain mustard
100g muscovado sugar
3 tbsp flaked sea salt
2 tbsp freshly ground
    black pepper
2 tsp smoked sweet paprika
1 tsp cayenne
2.5kg boned pork shoulder

For the barbecue sauce:
450g ketchup (see p.37, or use
    a good shop-bought brand)
100ml red wine vinegar
3 tbsp Worcestershire sauce
25g dark muscovado sugar
flaked sea salt and freshly
    ground black pepper, to taste

Make the barbecue sauce: pour the remaining braising liquid into a small pan, bring it to the boil over a medium heat, and let half of the liquid evaporate to give an even more concentrated flavour. Reduce the heat, add the remaining ingredients, stir until the sugar dissolves, and simmer for 10–15 minutes until thickened slightly.

Remove from the heat, taste and check the seasoning – you might need a little more salt and pepper to balance out the sweetness.

Reheat the shredded pork by adding it to the pan with the warm barbecue sauce and stirring it over a low heat until warmed through. Pile the juicy pork and barbecue sauce into the rolls or bread of your choice. Top with slices of pickled cucumber.

VARIATION: Use any leftover pork to create an incredible twist on shepherd's pie. Spoon it into a small pie dish or baking dish, top with a layer of fluffy mash, sprinkle over some cheese, and bake in a preheated oven at 180°C/gas mark 4 for about 30 minutes, until the meat is hot and bubbling, and the cheese is melted, golden and crusty on top.

TO FREEZE: The cooked pulled pork will freeze beautifully for up to two weeks. Defrost in the fridge overnight, then reheat gently in a pan.

For the pickled cucumbers:
18ml red wine vinegar
1 tbsp caster sugar
1½ tsp fine sea salt
3 whole black peppercorns
1 small garlic clove,
    thinly sliced
1 bay leaf
1 sprig of rosemary
200g cucumber, thinly sliced
½ onion, thinly sliced

To serve:
Cream Buns (see p.56), or
    sliced sourdough bread
    or brioche buns, other
    rolls or bread

Makes: 12

MEDITERRANEAN VEGETABLE COBBLER

Cobbler – a traditional American home-cooked pudding. We take the same idea and make it savoury with a rattatouille-like stew. It's heart-warming fare that's perfect for cooler weather.

After you try out this recipe, feel free to use the cobbler topping with almost any other casserole. Our version is vegetarian, but the dumplings would be delicious with any meat or fish stew too.

METHOD

Prepare the scone dough as in the recipe on p.133, cover the bowl of rough dough with cling film and keep it in the fridge until you need it.

To make the vegetable stew, heat half the olive oil in a large, deep frying pan and use it to cook the aubergine until golden brown on all sides. Drain the aubergine in a colander and leave it to one side, saving any oil that runs off. Return this oil to the frying pan to use again, with the rest of the oil to hand so you can top up the pan as you cook the rest of the vegetables. (You may need to add a little more as you go if the pan shows signs of becoming dry – don't stint on the oil here.)

Cook the celery and onion in the oil in a large casserole over a medium heat until they soften – 8-10 minutes – then add the red peppers and continue cooking, stirring from time to time until soft – 5-8 minutes more. Remember not to let the pan get dry. Now add the courgette – cook until softened and slightly golden, about 5 minutes. Add the garlic, thyme and chilli and cook, stirring, until they begin to give off their scent – a further 5 minutes. Throw in the cherry tomatoes and continue to cook until their skins begin to break down and they give out their juices. Add the capers and olives, then, after another 2 minutes, the canned tomatoes. Bring the mixture to the boil, add the oregano, taste, and season with salt and pepper. Reduce the heat and simmer for 15–20 minutes. You may need to add water at this point to reach the right consistency: you're looking for a very thick soup, rather than a stew. Every time you add water, return the vegetables to a simmer and check the seasoning. Finally, return the aubergines to the pan and stir them in gently.

INGREDIENTS

For the cobbler topping:
½ quantity uncooked Gruyère and chive scone dough (see p.133)

For the vegetables:
250ml olive oil
1 large aubergine, cut into 2cm cubes
3 celery sticks, roughly chopped
1 large red onion, sliced
2 large red peppers, seeded and roughly chopped
1 courgette, cut into 2cm cubes
5 garlic cloves, finely chopped
10 sprigs of thyme
1 small red chilli, seeded and finely chopped
250g cherry tomatoes, halved
50g pickled capers, drained
100g stoned black olives
400g can chopped tomatoes
1 tbsp dried oregano
2 tsp flaked sea salt
1 tsp freshly ground black pepper
small bunch of flat leaf parsley, stalks discarded, leaves roughly chopped
small bunch of basil, leaves only
1 lemon (zest and juice)

Serves: 8

Remove the vegetables from the heat and add the parsley, basil, lemon zest and lemon juice. Pour the vegetables into a deep baking dish large enough to hold all the mixture with 5cm left between the top of the stew and the top of the dish – 20cm x 30cm and 7cm deep is ideal.

Preheat the oven to 180°C/gas mark 4. Drop scoops of the chilled scone dough on top of the vegetables – about 11 dollops in total. Bake for 25–30 minutes, until the scones are a dark golden brown, and the vegetables are bubbling up around them. Serve with a green salad – no bread needed here.

TO MAKE IN ADVANCE: Pour the stew into the baking dish, wrap in cling film and chill overnight. The scone dough can also sit happily overnight in the fridge and be added just before baking.

SOURDOUGH LASAGNE

No pasta in the cupboard? Here's a version of a layered bread pie that has all the attributes of lasagne.

METHOD

Make the tomato sauce: heat the olive oil in a large pan. Fry the garlic briefly, for about a minute, taking care not to let it colour. Add the tomato purée and cook, stirring, for a couple of minutes, until it becomes darker and richer in colour. Add the tomatoes and the water and bring to the boil, then reduce the heat and simmer for 30 minutes. Taste and season with salt and pepper. Remove from the heat and add the basil leaves, leaving them whole, then set the pan aside.

Preheat your oven to 180°C/gas mark 4. Lay the slices of sourdough on a baking sheet and toast them in the oven until golden brown and completely dried out, without a speck of moisture left in them, about 10 minutes. Imagine them as giant croûtons and you're pretty much there. You'll need to flip them over and rotate the tray halfway through. Remove from the oven and set aside. Increase the oven temperature to 200°C/gas mark 6. Line a baking tray with baking paper, and spread the aubergine slices evenly across it. Drizzle them with olive oil and sprinkle over some salt, then bake, turning once, until soft to the point of a knife, and light golden brown, about 25 minutes. Remove from the oven and set aside. Repeat this with the courgette (about 20 minutes), fennel (about 30 minutes) and the peppers. The peppers in particular should be allowed to cook really well, so they're completely soft, with blackened, blistered skins, about 45 minutes. If you have lots of baking trays and space in your oven, you can roast more than one batch of vegetables at once, but the reason for cooking them separately is that they all cook at different speeds, so keep an eye on each lot. Don't switch off the oven, even after the vegetables are cooked. Once the peppers are roasted and soft, you'll need to remove their skins. Here's a trick we use at the bakery: put the peppers, still hot, into a large mixing bowl and cover the top tightly with cling film. By the time they've cooled, the skins should slip off easily.

Make the cheesy filling: blitz all the ingredients in a food processor, or stir energetically together with a wooden spoon, until completely combined.

INGREDIENTS

For the tomato sauce:
3 tbsp olive oil
1 garlic clove, thinly sliced
2 tbsp tomato purée
2 x 400g cans chopped tomatoes
250ml water
1 bunch of basil, leaves only
flaked sea salt and freshly
    ground black pepper, to taste

For the 'lasagne':
9 slices of sourdough bread,
    5mm thick
olive oil, for drizzling
    and greasing
1 aubergine, cut into 3cm slices
1 courgette, cut into 3cm slices
1 fennel bulb, cut into 3cm slices
3 red peppers, seeded,
    and halved

For the cheesy filling:
400g soft goat's cheese
200ml double cream
1 sprig of rosemary, leaves
    only, finely chopped
2 garlic cloves, crushed
1 tsp freshly ground
    black pepper
½ tsp fine sea salt

To finish:
100g Parmesan, grated

Serves: 8

Begin to assemble the dish: oil a deep baking dish that measures about 20cm x 30cm and lay three slices of sourdough inside to line the base. Pour over a layer of about a third of the tomato sauce to cover the bread thoroughly. Top this with a layer of about a third of the mixed roast vegetables, then dot over a third of the goat's cheese filling. Repeat twice more, until you've used all your bread, sauce, vegetables and filling, finishing with the goat's cheese mixture.

Bake for 45 minutes, or until bubbling and golden. Take briefly from the oven, scatter over the grated Parmesan, then pop back into the oven for 10 minutes or so, until the cheese has formed a gold crust on the top. A green salad is all you need with this.

LUNCH FOCACCIA

A great centrepiece for a buffet or lunch spread, this is almost like a giant, savoury layer cake, with all kinds of good things packed between two pieces of focaccia. Once sliced, it's very portable, so is well suited to picnics and packed lunches.

Save any leftover red pepper aioli in a sealed container in the fridge for another day, if you can resist eating it all straight away.

METHOD

Make the red pepper aioli first. Blitz the roasted, skinned pepper with the crushed garlic and basil in a food processor until you have a rough paste. Turn into a mixing bowl and gradually whisk in the mayonnaise, then set aside.

Preheat the oven to 220°C/gas mark 7. With a sharp, serrated knife, slice the focaccia in half to create two thinner sheets of bread. Drizzle the cut sides with olive oil and bake, cut sides up, for 5–7 minutes until the surface is golden and crisp. Leave to cool slightly, then spread generously with the aioli.

On one cut side that will form the 'base' of the sandwich, sprinkle over some rocket, then lay over the ham, the radishes and the sliced avocado. Shave over the manchego (or other cheese) using a vegetable peeler, then top with the strips of roast pepper. Season well with salt, pepper and lemon juice. Close up the 'sandwich' with the other half of the focaccia, and cut into 6–8 squares to serve.

INGREDIENTS

For the red pepper aioli:
1 large red pepper, roasted, skinned and seeded (see the Sourdough Lasagne recipe on p.160 for tips on roasting peppers)
1 garlic clove, crushed
2 sprigs of basil, leaves only
150g mayonnaise (homemade see p.36, or a top-quality brand)

For the focaccia:
1 Focaccia (see p.57)
100g rocket
100g cured ham, such as lomo, Serrano or Parma, thinly sliced
40g radishes, thinly sliced
1 ripe avocado, peeled, sliced thinly, and tossed in a little lemon juice
70g manchego, Parmesan or Pecorino
2 red peppers, roasted, skinned and torn into rough strips
flaked sea salt and freshly ground black pepper, to taste
1 lemon (juice only)
olive oil, for drizzling

Serves: 6–8

RICOTTA, LEMON AND SAGE BREAD PIE

This is a bread baker's take on the pastry chef's French classic, *Pithivier*. It's also a good alternative to a sandwich – another way to put delicious things between bread.

Using whole lemons, rind and all, gives the filling the very merest hint of bitterness – the kind that your mouth will thank you for. Slicing the fruit thinly and macerating it in the olive oil and salt reduces the lemon's tartness. Here, that perennial pairing of almonds and lemons – more common in sweet than savoury dishes – is used to full advantage. Really go for it and dark-roast your nuts to maximise the play of the flavours against each other. This is particularly good with a glass of wine – it also makes a welcome change in a packed lunch, or at a picnic: just slice and wrap.

METHOD

Stir together the lemon, sage, olive oil and salt and leave to marinade for at least an hour, or for up to two days. The longer timescale will give you more tender lemons and an even better flavour.

Take the spelt dough and shape it into a ball on a floured surface. Cut off a third of the dough. With a floured rolling pin, press this smaller piece out to a 20cm circle to form the base of your pie. Line a baking sheet with non-stick baking paper, and lay the pie base carefully onto it.

Stir together the ricotta, the salt and the Parmesan, then spoon onto the pie base, heaping it up in the centre and leaving a 3cm border around the edge. Top with the lemon mixture, then scatter over the almonds.

Roll out the remaining larger piece of dough to a 25cm circle and lay it over the base and filling. Press the edges of both pieces of dough together, like a giant ravioli, to secure the contents. Use your fingers to crimp all around the border to give a beautiful fluted effect. This is a very rustic dish, though, so don't get too caught up in the presentation.

Put the baking sheet and pie into a large plastic bag, inflated so that it won't come into contact with the dough, and leave the pie to rest on the worktop for 45 minutes. The dough will relax and puff up slightly, but you're not looking for it to rise hugely, and certainly not to double in size. Just before it's ready, preheat the oven to 170°C/gas mark 3. Brush the top of the pie lightly with water, and sprinkle the poppy seeds around the edge. Sit a few sage leaves in the centre as a garnish.

Bake the pie for about 45 minutes, until a rich golden brown. The base should be much darker than the top and cooked right through. Serve warm.

INGREDIENTS

For the filling:
1 unwaxed lemon, very thinly
    sliced – both flesh and rind
    (remove pips)
3 sprigs of sage, leaves only,
    roughly chopped
3 tbsp olive oil
150g ricotta
1 tsp flaked sea salt
40g Parmesan, finely grated
50g almonds, skin on, toasted
    (see p.35) and roughly
    chopped

For the bread parcel:
½ quantity spelt rolls dough
    (see p.55), after its first rise
flour, for dusting
olive oil, for brushing
1 tsp poppy seeds, for sprinkling
a few fresh sage leaves,
    for garnish

Serves: 4–6

ROOT VEGETABLE AND FONTINA BAKE

This is an incredibly rich way to introduce two of our favourite ingredients to your repertoire. One is more controversial than the other – an artichoke that's not really an artichoke at all. The Jerusalem artichoke is actually a relative of the sunflower, and the edible part is a tuberous root that's delicious both raw and cooked. Raw, it has a crisp freshness and can be added to salads shaved very finely, but it comes into its own when it is cooked very simply, especially roasted with olive oil and garlic. It also loves cream and cheese, making it perfect for a gratin. Fontina is an Italian cheese that melts beautifully at high temperatures, lending a pungent background note that has a pleasing whiff of the farmyard about it. Young Fontina is soft and milder, while the stronger, aged version is hard: either kind works here. As it melts, the root vegetables virtually cook in the liquid cheese, soaking up much of its flavour. The vegetables listed here are really only suggestions. You can play with whatever combination you choose, depending on what's in season and what you like best, as long as the total weight comes to about 1.5 kg.

METHOD

Grease a deep baking dish, about 20cm x 30cm with a little olive oil. Preheat the oven to 180°C/gas mark 4.

Prepare the seasoned salt by rubbing the thyme and garlic into the salt. Slice all the peeled vegetables into thin rounds, no more than 2mm thick.

Layer slices of vegetable into the dish, making sure that the layer uses a good mix of different veg. Drizzle lightly with olive oil. Sprinkle with the seasoned salt and lay two slices of Fontina side by side on the top. Add another layer of vegetables, another light drizzle of oil, followed by salt and cheese. Repeat the layers until you've used up all the ingredients, finishing up with a layer of vegetables rather than cheese. If the vegetables are beginning to tower up out of the baking dish, don't worry, they'll shrink down as they bake. Use a pastry brush to lightly coat the top layer with olive oil and sprinkle with a little more seasoned salt. Wrap the whole dish tightly in foil and bake for 1½ hours.

When nearly ready, make the topping. Remove the crusts from the bread and roughly tear into 1-2cm chunks. Put the torn bread in a bowl, drizzle over the maple syrup and toss together to moisten the bread, then toss through the remaining ingredients. Carefully take the dish out of the oven, unwrap it and scatter over the topping. Return it to the oven for a further 15–20 minutes until the topping has crisped up and turn a warm golden brown.

Serve warm straight from the dish, with a green salad for contrasting crunch.

INGREDIENTS

For the seasoned salt:
10 sprigs of thyme, leaves only, roughly chopped
3 garlic cloves, finely chopped
1 tbsp flaked sea salt

For the root vegetables:
olive oil, for greasing, drizzling and brushing
1 small sweet potato, peeled
1 golden beetroot, peeled
1 red beetroot, peeled
½ celeriac, peeled
2 Jerusalem artichokes, peeled
3 baby turnips, peeled
1 carrot, peeled
1 parsnip, peeled
1 small swede, peeled
300g Fontina, rind removed, thinly sliced

For the topping:
200g sourdough bread
50g maple syrup
2 tbsp Dijon mustard
2 tsp flaked sea salt
1 tsp freshly ground black pepper

Serves: 8

LEEK AND GOAT'S CHEESE PICNIC LOAF

This is a slightly zany, totally delicious idea for a picnic dish that makes a great alternative to sandwiches. It turns a hollowed-out loaf into a bread bowl, which is then filled like a quiche with a rich custard and plenty of fillings. Here, we used the French Dark Sourdough (see p.40). You can easily mix the fillings up to suit your tastes – just don't forget to pack a good serrated knife for cutting and serving.

METHOD

Preheat the oven to 180°C/gas mark 4. Prepare the bread bowl. Slice across the loaf of bread to remove the upper third, then use your hands to pull out as much of the middle of the remaining loaf as you can, creating a crusty bowl. You won't need this excavated bread for this recipe, so set it aside to make breadcrumbs.

Bake the bread bowl for 10 minutes, then, once it's cool enough to handle, gently rub the cut sides of garlic around the inside of the loaf. Coat the inside with mustard – use the back of a spoon or, even better, a pastry brush, to help you spread it evenly. Set the hollowed-out loaf aside and increase the oven temperature to 200°C/gas mark 6.

To make the filling, toss the leeks with the olive oil, salt, pepper and thyme and roast them for 30 minutes until meltingly soft. Leave to cool, then drain off any excess oil. In a separate jug, make the custard by whisking together the eggs and cream, then season well with salt and pepper.

Begin to assemble the loaf: place the bread bowl on a baking tray and spread the goat's cheese evenly on the base, then top with the leeks. Pour the eggs and cream into the bread bowl in three stages, waiting a few minutes each time before adding more. Once all the custard is added, carefully transfer to the oven. Bake for 10 minutes, then reduce the temperature to 170°C/gas mark 3 and bake for a further 25–35 minutes until the custard is set. Check the custard is cooked by inserting a skewer into the middle; if it comes out wet, give it another 5–10 minutes. Leave it to cool for 45 minutes to an hour. It should look rather like a quiche, and you can slice it up to serve it in just the same way.

VARIATIONS: As long as you stick to the same measurements for the savoury custard (the eggs and cream), anything goes – think of your favourite quiche and reinvent it as a picnic bread pie.

TO MAKE IN ADVANCE: This can be baked the day before you want to eat it. Reheat at 180°C/gas mark 4 for 10 minutes to bring it back to life before packing up and heading out on your picnic.

INGREDIENTS

1 round loaf of bread, 20–25cm in diameter – any kind you like
1 garlic clove, halved
2 tsp Dijon mustard
4 leeks, finely sliced, dark leaves discarded
100ml olive oil
½ tsp salt, plus extra to taste
½ tsp black pepper, plus extra to taste
5 sprigs of thyme, leaves only, chopped
2 eggs
150ml double cream
250g soft, fresh goat's cheese, crumbled

Serves: 6

TEA

TEATIME SANDWICHES

Sandwiches are such a regular part of our diet these days, that for many, they've lost some of their magic – quite unfairly. These three suggestions for teatime versions are dainty and delicate but full of flavour and texture, and couldn't be more different from the chunky, stodgy, refrigerated, pre-packed wedges devoured unthinkingly at desks every lunchtime. They're small, tempting and delicious and perfect for afternoon tea – which, after all, is a meal eaten out of greed rather than hunger, and for special occasions, so it's not as though you need to serve anything particularly filling.

You can use any of our loaves, thinly sliced, for these sandwiches or use little rolls – such as our spelt rolls or cream buns. You can make as few or as many as you like using the suggestions below.

ANCHOVY BUTTER AND RADISHES
Blitz a small, 50g can of anchovy fillets, drained of their oil, with 250g butter at room temperature. Use the best anchovies you can find – ideally Spanish. Spoon into a small container with sealable lid and chill until fairly firm but still spreadable. Spread thickly onto the bread. Scatter half the slices with crisp, fresh wedges of radishes – blush and white breakfast radishes if you can find them – then sandwich with the remaining anchovy-buttered bread. Serve cut in triangles or fingers. Any leftover anchovy butter can be stored in the fridge for several days.

CUCUMBER, MINT AND GOAT'S CURD
Mild, fresh goat's curd is in season in spring and early summer, but if you can't find it, use the softest, purest, youngest soft goat's cheese you can find. Spread it onto sliced bread and use a potato peeler to shave long, thin strips of cucumber in a tangle on top of half the slices. Tear over a few leaves of fresh mint and finish with a grind of black pepper and a squeeze of fresh lemon juice. Invert the remaining curd-spread bread slices over the cucumber. Serve cut in triangles or fingers.

EGG MAYONNAISE
Egg mayonnaise uses so few ingredients that they need to be the best you can find. Homemade mayonnaise is great, but good shop-bought will do well. Boil as many eggs as you need (one large will make 1½–2 rounds) until the yolks are only just firm – you don't want greying, powdery yolks. They should be almost gooey. Once cooked (7–8 minutes for large eggs at room temperature, a minute more if they're straight from the fridge), cool the eggs under running water until you can peel them comfortably. Mash roughly with a fork and stir in enough mayonnaise to give a rich mixture. Add salt, pepper and a knife-point of Dijon mustard. Chopped chives or spring onions elevate an egg mayonnaise sandwich even further.

SCONES

The secret to a light, airy, buttery scone is to keep the processing to a minimum. The more you handle the dough, the more you develop the gluten in the flour, and the harder the scone. Bear this in mind, keep your butter cold, and your scones will be as light as a feather – the perfect foil for jam, lemon curd, clotted cream or, simply, butter.

We like our scones generously sized, but if you prefer yours daintier, just use a smaller cutter.

METHOD

Preheat the oven to 170°C/gas mark 3. Sift the flour, salt and baking powder together into a large bowl. Tip in the cubes of cold butter and use your fingertips to rub the butter into the mixture until no large lumps of butter remain – a few small lumps of butter, however, are no bad thing. The result should resemble coarse breadcrumbs. Lastly, rub in the sugar.

Beat the milk and eggs together in a jug, then pour this into the flour mixture, stirring as you go. Bring everything together to form a rough dough, but don't over-mix or aim for anything too smooth, or your scones will end up tough.

Dust the worktop and rolling pin with flour and roll the dough out to a square, about 26cm x 26cm and roughly 3–4cm deep. Dip a round cutter about 8cm across into some flour and cut out nine scones. Use a smooth, swift motion with your cutter to ensure clean-cut edges – this helps your scones to rise. Gather up the leftover dough, roll it out again and cut out as many more as you can. You should get about a dozen large scones from this mixture. Transfer them to a baking sheet lined with non-stick baking paper.

With a soft pastry brush, paint the tops of the scones lightly with egg wash. Bake for about 20 minutes until risen and golden, with crusty tops and dark golden bases, which should sound hollow when tapped.

VARIATION: To make apple scones, cut 200g cored Bramley apple (skin left on) into 1.5cm dice, and toss through the flour mixture once all the butter and sugar is incorporated along with 100g currants. Add 2 teaspoons of natural vanilla extract and the grated zest of a lemon to the milk mixture. Top the glazed scones with a handful of flaked almonds before baking, and dust with icing sugar once cool.

INGREDIENTS

200g butter, chilled and diced
720g plain flour
½ tsp fine sea salt
3 tbsp baking powder
140g caster sugar
3 eggs
160ml milk
egg wash (see p.35)

Makes: about 12 large scones

BANANA, WALNUT AND MILK CHOCOLATE COOKIES

Chunky cookies full of goodies are the stuff of legend, and have become the base from which vast global empires have risen. But how did the humble homemade cookie make it across the globe? By persuading us that there's no difference between hand-made and factory made. Well, clearly we think there is, and this recipe proves it. And because cookies are an easy starting point for introducing children to the world of baking, this recipe is also a perfect opportunity to teach kids what that difference means. The sugars you choose to use will make a big difference to your cookies. The more brown sugar you include, the chewier they'll be. Moisteners play their part too – here you get them from the banana and the egg. Finally, though, everything comes down to the baking. We like our cookies chewy, but prefer not to under-bake them. This recipe allows you to cook them right through and get all the rich, caramelised flavours that brings, but still leaves you with gorgeous, yielding centres. Chilling is also important – it affects both the cookies' texture and their flavour. If you have the opportunity, prepare the dough the day before, as it really does benefit from a night spent in the fridge.

These aren't as extravagantly big as some American-style cookies: they're a little more modestly-sized and manageable for children – and anyway, you can always have two!

METHOD

Sift together the wholemeal flour, plain flour, salt, cinnamon and bicarbonate of soda into a large bowl. Tip any bran caught in the sieve back into the bowl with the rest of the dry ingredients.

In a stand mixer fitted with the beater, or with a handmixer in a large bowl, beat the butter at high speed until white and creamy. Add the caster sugar and muscovado sugar and cream until light and fluffy. Add the egg and the vanilla, beating all the while. Reduce the speed to medium and mix in the mashed bananas, then reduce the speed to low and mix while you add the flour mixture, then the oats, the chocolate chunks and the chopped walnuts, until well combined. Cover the bowl with cling film and chill the dough for at least 1 hour, or overnight.

When you're ready to bake, line two baking sheets with non-stick baking paper, then form the dough into 30 balls. Each should weigh about 30g – weigh the first one to get an idea of the right size and use it as a guide while you form the rest. Space these well apart on the baking sheets and push down to flatten very slightly – they will spread further as they cook. Cover with a sheet of baking paper and chill for a final 30 minutes while you preheat the oven to 170°C/gas mark 3. Bake for 15–20 minutes, until the edges are crisp and golden but the centres are still soft. Leave to cool on the baking sheets for at least 15 minutes before transferring to a wire rack. They are fantastic when eaten still warm.

INGREDIENTS

60g wholemeal flour
110g plain flour
½ tsp fine sea salt
½ tsp ground cinnamon
½ tsp bicarbonate of soda
140g butter, at room temperature
70g caster sugar
90g light muscovado sugar
1 egg
1 tsp natural vanilla extract
1 very ripe large banana, mashed
80g rolled oats
170g milk chocolate, chopped into rough chunks
60g walnuts, toasted (see p.35) and roughly chopped

Makes: 30 cookies

CHOCOLATE CHIP COOKIES

Years of tasting and testing (gruelling work, that) have finally led us to what we think is the perfect chocolate chip cookie: a bit chewy, a bit gooey, just crisp around the edges and packed with rich, almost caramel notes that complement the masses of chocolate. As well as the all-important mix of brown and white sugars, salt is crucial to the flavour of a good chocolate chip cookie. Chilling the dough not only makes it easier to handle but also does something magical to the flavour. An hour is the minimum, but a full night in the fridge would be ideal. In our bakeries we sell giant cookies (see p.178–9 for photograph), almost the size of your head and good for sharing. A domestic oven doesn't have the space to bake them, so this recipe is for more manageable, smaller cookies.

METHOD

Sift together the flour, bicarbonate of soda and salt into a large bowl. In a stand mixer fitted with the beater, or with a handmixer in a large bowl, beat the butter at high speed until pale and creamy. Add the caster sugar and muscovado sugar and cream until light and fluffy. Add the egg, egg yolk and the vanilla, beating all the while. Reduce the speed to very low and add the flour mixture, beating until well combined. Finally, stir through the chunks of chocolate. Cover the bowl with cling film and chill for at least 1 hour or, ideally, overnight. When you're ready to bake, line two baking sheets with non-stick baking paper, then form the dough into 30 balls. Each should weigh about 30g – measure out the first one carefully and use it as a guide. Space these well apart on the baking sheets and push down on their tops to flatten very slightly – they will spread further as they cook. Cover with a sheet of baking paper and chill for a final 30 minutes while you preheat the oven to 170°C/gas mark 3. Bake for 15–20 minutes, until the edges are crisp and golden but the centres are still soft. Leave to cool a little, but not too much, before eating. Nothing beats a warm chocolate chip cookie – except a warm chocolate chip cookie and a glass of cold milk (one of the most popular desserts we serve at GAIL's Kitchen).

VARIATION: You can make a giant cake-sized cookie using half this mixture. Butter and line a 20cm iron skillet or cake tin with baking paper. Press the dough evenly down into the base and bake as above for 30–35 minutes. Leave it to cool, then carefully turn it out. Decorate to your heart's desire, and cut into slices to serve. Children go crazy for this – there's something about a giant cookie that they just love (adults too!).

TO FREEZE: Freeze the shaped balls of dough in an airtight container, you can then bake them straight from the freezer whenever the need for fresh cookies strikes. Just allow them a little longer in the oven.

INGREDIENTS

220g plain flour
1 tsp bicarbonate of soda
¾ tsp fine sea salt
170g butter, at room
    temperature
110g caster sugar
80g light muscovado sugar
1 egg, plus 1 egg yolk
1 tsp natural vanilla extract
200g dark chocolate (at least
    70 per cent cocoa), chopped
    into rough chunks

Makes: 30 cookies

OAT, PECAN AND CRANBERRY COOKIES

These nubbly biscuits are somewhere between a flapjack and cookie, with crisp edges and soft, crumbly centres.

The classic oat and raisin cookie was always screaming for a slightly sour note. After playing with various combinations, we found that dried cranberries gave the bright, tart touch we craved. The best kind have no added sugar for a really fresh flavour, so go to the trouble to seek them out. This recipe would work equally well with dried sour cherries, or even with chopped prunes for a more mysterious, darker note. Pecans are particularly gorgeous with oats, but even this combination isn't gospel. If you don't have them use whatever is to hand – walnuts, blanched hazelnuts, or almonds.

At GAIL's we make our cookies family-sized (see p.179 for photograph) but these smaller versions are more manageable in a domestic oven.

METHOD

Sift together the flour, baking powder and salt into a large bowl, then stir in the pecans, cranberries and oats.

In the bowl of a stand mixer fitted with the paddle attachment, or in a large bowl with a hand mixer, beat the butter at high speed until pale and creamy. Add the sugars and beat until light, very pale and fluffy. Add the egg and the vanilla, and beat until well combined.

Stop the mixer and tip all the dry ingredients into the bowl. Mix at low speed until only just combined. Cover the bowl with cling film and chill for at least 1 hour.

When you're ready to bake, line two baking sheets with non-stick baking paper, then form the dough into 30 balls. Each should weigh about 30g – weigh the first one to get an idea of the right size and use it as a guide while you form the rest. Space these well apart on the baking sheets and push down to flatten very slightly – they will spread further as they cook. Cover with a sheet of baking paper and chill for a final 30 minutes while you preheat the oven to 170°C/gas mark 3. Place the cookies in the oven and bake for 15–20 minutes. Their edges should be a crisp golden brown, but the centres should be puffed up and cakey, not baked hard. These are gorgeous when fresh out the oven and still warm, but if you can resist, they'll keep for a few days in an airtight container.

TO FREEZE: Freeze the shaped balls of dough in an airtight container, you can then bake them straight from the freezer whenever the need for fresh cookies strikes. Just allow them a little longer in the oven.

INGREDIENTS

140g plain flour
1 tsp baking powder
½ tsp fine sea salt
110g pecans, toasted and
  roughly chopped (see p.35
  for how to toast nuts)
80g dried cranberries,
  roughly chopped
200g rolled oats
170g butter, at room
  temperature
90g light muscovado sugar
180g caster sugar
1 egg, at room temperature
1 tsp natural vanilla extract

Makes: 30 cookies

GINGERBREAD BISCUITS

Ginger, just like chilli, is a hot spice. It literally warms you up, so no wonder its flavour evokes the winter season like nothing else. At Christmas we make gingerbread decorations for our bakeries, and bake tiny gingerbread men to top our Christmas cupcakes (and decapitate them for Halloween!). This is the perfect gingerbread biscuit for building a gingerbread house or making tree decorations – it works with all kinds of intricate shapes.

We like properly spicy gingerbread that you can really feel going down the back of your throat. The white pepper in this recipe enhances the other warming flavours. You could swap the golden syrup for honey for a more old-fashioned biscuit, or, to take the spicy, almost savoury flavours even further, use black treacle. To pack a seriously gingery punch, use the syrup from a jar of preserved stem ginger.

METHOD

Sift together the flour, spices and bicarbonate of soda into a large bowl then scatter over the cubes of cold butter. Use your fingertips to rub the butter into the flour mixture until it resembles coarse breadcrumbs, with no large lumps of butter left. Stir in the muscovado sugar.

In a separate bowl beat the egg into the golden syrup with a fork, then add to the flour mixture and stir well until combined. You will have a soft dough. Form into a rough rectangle, wrap in cling film and chill for at least 1 hour, or overnight.

When you're ready to bake, preheat the oven to 170°C/gas mark 3. Lightly dust the worktop and a rolling pin with flour and roll out the chilled dough to a thin sheet, 3–5mm thick. Dip your cutter lightly in flour and cut out as many shapes as possible from the dough, rekneading and rolling as necessary. Bake for 10–15 minutes until just crisp. Smaller sizes will need less time, fans of crispy biscuits should leave for longer. As the dough is already dark; it's difficult to judge these for doneness by colour, so if you're really keen to get your timing spot on, make one biscuit, let it cool completely and use it as a gauge. These keep very well in an airtight container for up to a week.

INGREDIENTS

440g plain flour, plus extra
    for dusting
1 tbsp ground ginger
1 tsp mixed spice
½ tsp ground white pepper
½ tsp ground cinnamon
1 tsp bicarbonate of soda
125g butter, chilled and diced
220g light muscovado sugar
1 egg
75g golden syrup

Makes: about 25 biscuits, depending on size and shape

PECAN BROWNIES

A glance at this list of ingredients and two things jump out at you: the salt, and the two types of chocolate – well, three, really, if you include the cocoa powder.

We adore dark bitter chocolate and could happily use the 70 per cent all the way through for a very grown-up brownie. At GAIL's, we use a crowd-pleasing combination of very dark and slightly less intense chocolate. You could use all 50 per cent chocolate if you prefer – perhaps if you're baking for children.

Where texture's concerned, the debate over cakey vs. fudgy brownies will probably rage on forever. We like ours fudgy, so we introduce as little air to the mixture as possible, beating the eggs and sugar just until the sugar dissolves. If you're in the cakey camp, whisk the eggs and sugar thoroughly until pale and doubled in volume, then fold into the mixture carefully to avoid knocking out the air.

These are best made the day before you want to eat them.

METHOD

Preheat the oven to 170°C/gas mark 3. Line a baking dish or brownie tray about 20cm x 30cm with baking paper.

Melt the butter and chocolate in a small heatproof bowl fitted snugly over the top of a small pan of gently simmering water, making sure that its base doesn't actually touch the water. Stir carefully until melted and combined, remove the bowl from the pan and beat in the cocoa powder. Pour into a very large mixing bowl and set aside to cool slightly.

Sift the flour into a bowl, add the salt and set aside. Whisk the eggs and both sugars together in another bowl, until the sugars have dissolved. Stir the eggs into the chocolate mixture, then fold in the flour, ensuring it's completely combined to give a smooth, glossy batter.

Pour the brownie mixture into the lined baking dish. Scatter the pecan halves generously across the surface, and bake for anything between 15 and 30 minutes. When ready, a small crack will have formed around the edges of the brownie, and the centre will still be a little wobbly. A skewer pushed into the centre should come out with large, gooey crumbs on it, but not coated in wet batter.

Leave the brownie to cool in its tin, then wrap the tin in cling film and chill overnight before cutting and devouring. This does demand serious willpower, but will give you the ultimate brownie – it's worth the wait.

INGREDIENTS

170g butter
200g very dark chocolate
(at least 70 per cent cocoa
solids), chopped into rough
chunks
100g dark chocolate
(50 per cent cocoa solids),
chopped into rough chunks
45g cocoa powder
(100 per cent cocoa solids)
130g plain flour
1 tsp flaked sea salt
5 eggs
200g caster sugar
120g light muscovado sugar
80g pecan halves

Makes: 12 brownies

HAZELNUT, HONEY AND BROWN BUTTER FINANCIERS

These classic French cakelets have been around for centuries, unchanged. You don't alter a winning recipe, and this one is a winner. Financiers are now found the world over, and when you bite into a good one you'll understand why. They're simple to make – but, even more so than in other recipes, the final result is wholly dependent on the quality of your ingredients. When a recipe contains so few components, every single one has a crucial role to play. Creating brown butter, for example, introduces even richer, more complex tones.

Financiers are normally baked in special moulds, now widely available in most good quality kitchen shops, and easily obtained online. They come in a large assortment of sizes and shapes. Choose one with small indents. A non-stick mini muffin tin will do just as well, and is probably easier to find – or you could use tartlet tins.

METHOD

Butter 12 financier moulds or tartlet tins very lightly.

Make the brown butter. Melt the cubes of butter in a saucepan over a low heat. When it begins to foam, scoop off the froth with a spoon to remove the impurities. As it continues to cook, the butter should turn a pale brown colour. Eventually, once you've scooped off all the foam, you'll be left with a clear, dark amber liquid. Pour into a clean bowl and leave to cool, but not to solidify. If it does solidify, reheat very gently until melted again.

Meanwhile, preheat the oven to 180°C/gas mark 4. Put the whole almonds and hazelnuts into the food processor along with the flour. Blitz to a fine powder. Decant this into a mixing bowl. With a balloon whisk, whisk in the icing sugar until well combined, then pour over the liquid brown butter. Stir well with a wooden spoon, then add the egg whites and stir together thoroughly. Finally, stir in the honey. Scoop the smooth mixture into the moulds or tins. Bake for 12–15 minutes until golden brown and springy. Cool in the tins before turning out.

VARIATIONS: For an added boozy punch, brush the cakes with dark rum or Amaretto as soon as they come out the oven, so they drink up all the liquid.

INGREDIENTS

150g butter, at room temperature, diced, plus extra for greasing
150g icing sugar
40g blanched almonds, toasted (see p.35 for toasting nuts)
40g blanched hazelnuts, toasted
60g plain flour
4 egg whites, lightly beaten
25g clear honey

Makes: 12 little cakes

RHUBARB AND CUSTARD TARTLETS

A classic flavour combo, this, and for good reason: tart, refreshing rhubarb against sweet, comforting vanilla custard. The crumble topping introduces yet another welcome contrast – that of crunch. (See p.186 for photograph.)

METHOD

Begin by making the rhubarb filling. Place the rhubarb in a saucepan, shake over the sugar, and add the lemon juice. Heat slowly, so that the rhubarb gives up its juices as the sugar dissolves. When the rhubarb is soft, begin to stir occasionally until you have a light compôte, but not so that the rhubarb breaks down completely – you want it to retain some of its shape. Transfer to a bowl, leave to cool, then cover and chill completely.

Remove the sweet almond pastry from the fridge. Lightly flour the worktop and rolling pin, then roll the dough out thinly to a thickness of 3mm. Take a 9cm round cutter (or larger, if you are using larger tartlet tins), dip it lightly in flour, and cut out 12 rounds of dough. Line 12 5cm tartlet tins with the dough: make sure that the dough is pressed down well around the base and sides of the tin, but don't worry about trimming the tops neatly – we think irregular edges only add to the charm of these tartlets. Put all the pastry cases into the freezer for about 30 minutes to firm up. Meanwhile, preheat the oven to 180°C/gas mark 4.

Fill the chilled tartlets with the chilled pastry cream. Drop a few chunks of rhubarb on top of each, then finish with a good topping of crumble. Bake for 20–25 minutes, until the pastry is cooked through, pale golden and crisp, and the crumble is golden.

INGREDIENTS

200g rhubarb, chopped
   into 2cm lengths
40g sugar
2 tbsp lemon juice
½ quantity sweet almond
   pastry, chilled (see p.33)
1 quantity pastry cream,
   chilled (see p.34),
½ quantity crumble topping
   (see p.32)
flour, for dusting

Makes: 12 mini tartlets,
   5cm in diameter

CHOCOLATE AND CUSTARD TARTLETS

Hamantaschen are typical little biscuits eaten at Purim, a festival that celebrates the delivery of the Jewish people from the Persian Empire. As with so many Jewish festivals, food is absolutely central, and giving gifts of food is an important part of celebrating Purim, along with feasting – and plenty of wine. Traditionally, hamantaschen are made with a poppy seed filling, but we wanted to make a more cosmopolitan version, so we started baking them with custard and chocolate instead. They instantly became so wildly popular that they completely eclipsed the original. These tarts evolved out of those biscuits – we've used the same dough and the same filling, but made them in a different shape.

METHOD

Take the sweet almond pastry out of the fridge. Lightly flour your worktop and rolling pin, then roll the dough out to a thickness of 3mm. Take a round 9cm cutter, dip it lightly in flour, and cut out 12 rounds of dough. Line 12 5cm tartlet tins with the dough: make sure that the dough is pressed down well around the base and sides of the tin, but don't worry about trimming the tops neatly – we think irregular edges only add to the charm of these tartlets. Put all the pastry cases into the freezer for about 30 minutes to firm up. Meanwhile, preheat the oven to 180°C/gas mark 4.

Fill the chilled tartlets with the chilled pastry cream. Top each with a generous helping of chocolate chunks, pressing them into the pastry cream, and bake the tartlets for 20–25 minutes, until the pastry is crisp, cooked through and pale golden. The chocolate will have melted and run into the vanilla cream to make an irresistible custard. Leave to cool before serving.

INGREDIENTS

½ quantity sweet almond pastry, chilled (see p.33)
1 quantity of pastry cream, chilled (see p.34)
100g dark chocolate, chopped into medium chunks
flour for dusting

Makes: 12 mini tartlets, 5cm in diameter

APRICOT AND PISTACHIO TARTLETS

Fresh apricots must be the most tantalising fruit on earth. They have such a short season and if you buy them anything less than perfectly ripe, they can be a bit of a let-down. One minute they're sour and far from ready to eat, and the next they're over-ripe and pappy. But introduce slightly under-ripe apricots to a little heat and they're transformed, making them fabulous in cakes and tarts as well as jams. Should you find yourself with apricots that are too firm and tangy to eat, the chance of them ripening into perfect sweetness may be remote, but all is not lost: their sour note is absolutely perfect for these tarts.

METHOD

First make the pistachio cream: blitz the sugar with the pistachios in a food processor until you have a fine powder. Add the butter and whizz for a moment until soft. Take a second to scrape the mixture down the sides of the bowl, add the egg, blitz, scrape again, then add the flour and cornflour. Mix until combined. Transfer the pistachio cream to a bowl, cover, and chill.

Take the sweet almond pastry out of the fridge. Lightly flour the worktop and rolling pin, then roll the dough out thinly to a thickness of 3mm. Take a 9cm round cutter, dip it lightly in flour, and cut out 12 rounds of dough. Line 12 5cm tartlet tins with the dough: make sure that the dough is pressed down well around the base and sides of the tin, but don't worry about trimming the tops neatly – irregular edges only add to the charm of these tartlets. Put the pastry cases into the freezer for about 30 minutes to firm up. Meanwhile, preheat the oven to 180°C/gas mark 4.

Fill the chilled tartlets with pistachio cream, perch two quarters of apricot on top, and sprinkle over the roughly chopped pistachios. Bake for 20–25 minutes, until the pastry is cooked through and crisp, and the bases of the tartlets are dark golden. Leave to cool, then dust with icing sugar just before serving.

VARIATIONS: You can swap almonds (skins on) for the pistachios, or use raspberries instead of apricots. In fact, almost any stone fruit or berry will work well here – cherries and pistachios are a particularly good combination.

INGREDIENTS

For the pistachio cream:
70g caster sugar
70g pistachios
70g butter, at room temperature
1 egg
10g plain flour
10g cornflour

For the tartlets:
½ quantity sweet almond pastry, chilled (see p.33)
6 apricots, stones removed, cut into quarters
60g pistachios, roughly chopped
icing sugar, for dusting

Makes: 12 tartlets, 5cm in diameter

LEMON CURD AND MASCARPONE TARTLETS WITH STRAWBERRIES

These tarts are built on strong foundations: the buttery base is simple, quick, forgiving, and hard to get wrong, but still gives a professional-looking result. It's a traditional recipe from Brittany, a region famed for both its butter and its sea salt, and here they combine to great effect. Salt always helps to make the sweet taste even sweeter. However, if you'd prefer to reduce the salt slightly, then your tarts won't suffer for it.

Homemade lemon curd is infinitely superior to the shop-bought variety, so if you go to the trouble of making it, make plenty (you can easily double this recipe – it will keep for a week in the fridge). It's delicious on toast or scones, for example. In this recipe, we play the sweet tartness of the curd off against creamy mascarpone to great effect. They love each other to bits. This recipe makes more pastry than you will need but you can keep it, covered, in the fridge for up to 3 days, or frozen for up to 2 weeks.

The strawberries on top are a final flourish – if you don't have strawberries, try any other fresh fruit you have to hand.

METHOD

The lemon curd should be made the day before you want to bake the tarts. Warm the lemon juice with half the sugar in a small saucepan until the sugar has dissolved. In a separate bowl, whisk the remaining sugar with the cornflour. In yet another bowl, whisk the eggs together, then continue whisking as you add the cornflour and sugar. By this stage, the lemon juice should be coming to the boil. When it does, pour it slowly onto the eggs, whisking all the while, then return the whole thing to the saucepan and bring back to the boil. Once you see bubbles appear, cook for a minute more, then take straight off the heat and strain through a fine sieve into a clean bowl. Cover with cling film, pressing it right down so that it touches the whole surface of the curd – this will prevent a skin from forming. When warm to the touch but not hot enough to melt the butter on first contact, whisk in the soft butter a lump at a time. Cover again with cling film and, when cold, chill in the fridge overnight to set.

Next, prepare the biscuit base. Tip the butter, icing sugar and salt into a food processor and blitz until you have a smooth cream. Add the egg yolks and blitz a moment more. Alternatively beat thoroughly in a bowl with a wooden spoon or use a hand beater. Sift together the baking powder and the flour, add to the buttery cream, and mix just a little longer until well combined.

Continued overleaf

INGREDIENTS

For the lemon curd:
100ml lemon juice
85g caster sugar
1 tbsp cornflour
2 eggs
100g butter, at room
    temperature

**For the salted butter
    biscuit base:**
150g butter
140g icing sugar
1 tsp salt
3 egg yolks
2 tsp baking powder
200g plain flour, plus extra
    for dusting

For the mascarpone cream:
½ vanilla pod
300g mascarpone cheese,
    at room temperature
50g icing sugar
150ml whipping cream

For the topping:
a large punnet of ripe
    strawberries, hulled
    and sliced
icing sugar, for dusting

Makes: 8 tartlets, 9cm in
    diameter

The pastry will be very soft. Scrape the dough out of the food processor onto cling film, wrap and chill for at least 2 hours, or overnight, until quite firm.

Remove the dough from the fridge. Lightly flour the worktop and rolling pin, then roll the dough out thinly to a thickness of 2–3mm. Take a 9cm round cutter, dip it lightly in flour, and cut out 8 rounds of dough. Sit the rounds snugly into the base of 8 fluted 9cm tartlet tins, but don't push the dough up around the sides. Chill the tartlet bases in the fridge for about 30 minutes to firm up. Meanwhile, preheat the oven to 180°C/gas mark 4.

Bake the chilled tartlet cases for 15–17 minutes until they turn a deep golden brown. Don't be afraid to bake them slightly longer than you think they need – they're so rich that they won't dry out. You will start to smell the combination of well-baked butter and sugar, which, combined with the contrast of the salt, is so central to this recipe. Leave them to cool in their tins on a wire rack, then turn out.

While the tartlet bases cool, make the mascarpone cream. Split open the vanilla pod with a sharp knife and use the blade to scrape the seeds into a large mixing bowl. Add the mascarpone and the sugar, and beat with wooden spoon until smooth. Whip the cream separately with a balloon whisk until it falls in soft folds, holds gentle peaks, and has tripled in size. Carefully fold the whipped cream into the mascarpone using a large, metal spoon.

Spread the mascarpone cream on top of the cooled tartlet bases, building up to a slight peak in which you can form a well. Drop a spoonful of lemon curd into this little hollow, then top with a generous tumble of sliced strawberries and dust with icing sugar. Once assembled, eat relatively quickly.

VARIATIONS: These tart bases will happily hold all manner of toppings. You could swap the lemon curd for a compôte – or even just top them with good jam for the ultimate in simplicity. If you have perfect, ripe soft fruit, it might be all you need: use whole berries or just slice or chop stoned fruits, then pile, no other distractions, onto the tart bases and dust with icing sugar. Try sprinkling on toasted chopped nuts, or flaked almonds.

TO MAKE IN ADVANCE: The lemon curd is best made the day before. The biscuit base, too, is best made the day before so it has plenty of time to chill.

SOURDOUGH AND CURRANT TART

Here's a very old-fashioned, very English recipe, with its dried fruits and fragrant spices, and its clever way of turning something simple into something luxurious. In this tart day-old breadcrumbs do exactly the same job as stale bread in bread and butter pudding.

METHOD

First, make the pastry. In the bowl of a stand mixer fitted with the beater, beat the butter until smooth and soft. Stop the mixer, scrape down the bowl, and add the cornflour, egg yolk, water, salt and sugar. Mix again on low speed until a soft paste forms. Stop, scrape down and add the flour, then mix slowly until you have a soft dough. Flatten out into a thick disc and wrap in cling film. Chill for 2 hours, or overnight.

Halve the pastry, wrap one half and store to use another day. Roll out the other half on a lightly floured surface to a 3mm thick disc. Use it to line a 24cm tart tin and bake blind (see p.31).

Preheat the oven to 170°C/gas mark 3, then make the filling. Just-cover the currants and sultanas with boiling water in a bowl. Leave to soak until they become juicy and plump – about 10 minutes – then pour off the water and pat them dry with kitchen paper. Toss the plump fruit with the breadcrumbs and half the grated nutmeg and set aside.

Meanwhile, put the cream and strips of lemon rind into a large pan and slowly bring to the boil. Remove from the heat. Fish out the rind – you won't need it anymore. Add the fruit and breadcrumb mixture to the warm cream and stir in well, leave to cool to room temperature.

In a separate bowl, beat the butter with a wooden spoon until smooth, then add the sugar and carry on beating until the mixture is light and fluffy. Swap your wooden spoon for a balloon whisk and whisk in the eggs, one at a time, then add the vanilla and brandy. Add the cream and currant mixture and stir in with the wooden spoon until completely combined.

Pour the filling into the cooled pastry case. Sprinkle it lightly with the demerara sugar and the remaining nutmeg. Dot with small flakes of butter – just enough to ensure that every mouthful will have a light, buttery topping. Bake for 30 minutes until just set, with a slight jiggle left in the centre. Serve slightly warm, with a jug of double cream for everyone to help themselves.

INGREDIENTS

For the pastry:
120g butter, at room temperature
60g cornflour
1 egg yolk
2 tbsp water
½ tsp fine sea salt
1 tsp caster sugar
130g plain flour, plus extra for dusting

For the filling:
90g currants
90g sultanas
120g fresh breadcrumbs
½ tsp freshly grated nutmeg
430ml double cream
1 lemon (rind only – peel it off in strips with a vegetable peeler)
80g butter, diced, at room temperature, plus extra for dotting
80g caster sugar
3 eggs, at room temperature
½ tsp natural vanilla extract
2 tbsp brandy
1 tbsp demerara sugar

Serves: 8

QUEEN OF TARTS

A reworking of that classic British dessert, Queen of Puddings, this tart depends on a balance of flavours and textures: the comforting consistency of the breadcrumb custard at the bottom; the pillowy, dreamy meringue on top and, in between, something seriously tart to provide a much-needed contrast. Think of the refreshing acidity of raspberries, gooseberries or rhubarb, or plums and apricots just the wrong side of ripe. Here we've opted for a plum or apricot compôte, but vary the recipe to fit your mood and the season. We've chosen to make Swiss meringue: it's the most foolproof method and gives the best result. The most important thing when making meringue is to ensure the sugar dissolves completely into the egg whites. The Swiss method calls for you to warm the egg whites and the sugar together before you whip them, as the heat helps the process along. It avoids any graininess, and helps prevent the meringue from 'weeping' as it bakes. A final note on the bay leaf in the custard – this is a very traditional British touch. Its flavour is subtle and only just noticeable, but well worth including.

METHOD

Preheat the oven to 170°C/gas mark 3. Begin by making the custard layer: in a large pan using a hand whisk, mix together all the ingredients except the brandy and egg yolks, and gently bring to the boil over a medium heat. Reduce the heat to low and simmer for 5 minutes. Remove from the heat and discard the bay leaf. Leave to cool slightly, then stir in the brandy. You'll have something like a thick porridge. Finally, whisk in the egg yolks.

Pour the warm, bread custard into the pre-baked tart case and bake for 20–30 minutes until just set and cooked through. Remove from the oven and leave to cool to room temperature, but leave the oven on.

Meanwhile, make the compôte. Stir all the ingredients together in a small pan and cook over a low heat until the sugar dissolves, then increase the heat and bring to the boil. Simmer for 5–8 minutes until the fruit breaks up and the compôte reduces slightly to a very soft jam-like, syrupy consistency. Remove from the heat and set aside to cool, then spoon all over the bread custard and spread it in an even layer up to the edges of the tart case.

Next, make the meringue: whisk the egg whites together very lightly with the caster sugar in a glass or metal bowl that will sit snugly over a saucepan. Half-fill the pan with water, but not enough so that it will touch the bowl on top of it, then bring to a simmer. Sit the bowl over the pan and continue to gently whisk the whites and sugar together. You're not aiming to incorporate any air here, just to heat the sugar until it dissolves. If you can rub the mixture between thumb and forefinger and not feel any graininess, you're there.

INGREDIENTS

For the custard layer:
120g fresh breadcrumbs
420ml double cream
150ml milk
1 bay leaf
1 lemon (finely grated zest)
pinch of fine sea salt
55g caster sugar
2 tbsp brandy
3 egg yolks

For the tart case:
1 x 24cm baked sweet almond tart
    case (see p.33 for the pastry
    and p.31 for how to blind-bake)

For the compôte layer:
150g plums or apricots, stoned
    and quartered
2 tbsp lemon juice
50g caster sugar
10g fresh root ginger, peeled
    and finely grated (for plums)
    or 1 tsp dried lavender (for
    apricots)

For the meringue topping:
4 egg whites
240g caster sugar

Serves: 8

Take off the heat and transfer the mixture into the spotlessly clean bowl of a stand mixer fitted with the whisk (to be completely certain it's free from grease and grime, you can wipe it with a few drops of lemon juice). Whisk on medium speed – you'll notice steam coming off the meringue as it cools. Continue until you have a thick, white, shiny, glossy meringue that holds stiff peaks.

Spoon the meringue mixture all over the compôte, building it up into a good mountain of meringue. With a small palette knife or a butter knife, swirl the meringue into whatever shapes you like. This is a lot of meringue for one tart – but that's half the fun.

Bake for 15–20 minutes until the meringue turns the colour of a very milky latte, with a crispy skin but a soft and mallowy middle.

Leave the tart to cool for at least an hour before serving. Slice using a hot knife to cut neatly through the meringue (run it under a very hot tap and dry the blade quickly).

LEMON DRIZZLE CAKE

You'll need a fair few lemons to make this cake. How many depends on the quality of your lemons, and the time of year (they're generally juicier in winter). You'll need at least three, possibly five, to get enough juice. If you do use more than three lemons, don't waste the zest of the extra fruit, even though the cake only calls for the zest of three. The lemon syrup will only benefit from a little extra zest if you have it to hand.

METHOD

Butter two loaf tins about 19cm x 8cm, or one large loaf tin measuring 24cm x 10cm, then line with non-stick baking paper. Preheat the oven to 200°C/gas mark 6.

For the cake, in a large mixing bowl, whisk the eggs and the sugar together with a balloon whisk until just combined, then add the sour cream, lemon juice and lemon zest. In a separate bowl, sift together the flour, salt and baking powder. Add the ground almonds to the sifted flour, then add this to the eggs and sugar and whisk to combine. Pour in the melted butter and whisk one final time.

Pour the batter evenly into the two cake tins or one large tin. Place in the oven, then immediately. Reduce the temperature to 170°C/gas mark 3. Bake for 30–40 minutes (for two small cakes) or 35–45 minutes (for one large cake) until a skewer inserted into the centres comes out clean, and the cake(s) are golden and springy to the touch.

While the cakes are baking, prepare the lemon syrup: put the sugar and lemon juice into a saucepan over a medium heat, gently simmer until all the sugar has dissolved. Set aside.

As soon as the cake(s) are ready and the instant you take them out of the oven, spike them all over using a skewer – at least 8–10 times per cake. Spoon the syrup generously all over them to soak them in their tins – you might need to do this in stages, to give the cakes time to absorb the liquid. Leave them to sit and cool in their tins, so they soak up all the syrup.

Continued overleaf

INGREDIENTS

For the cake(s):
5 eggs
300g caster sugar
170g sour cream
50ml lemon juice
3 lemons (finely grated zest)
230g plain flour
1 tsp fine sea salt
2 tsp baking powder
50g ground almonds
150g butter, melted but not hot

For the lemon syrup:
65ml lemon juice
75g caster sugar

For the lemon icing:
200g icing sugar, sifted
40ml lemon juice

Makes: 1 large or 2 small
   loaf cakes

While the cake(s) cool, make the lemon icing: mix the sifted icing sugar with the lemon juice in a small bowl, using a fork or a wooden spoon, until smooth. The consistency should be liquid enough to drip elegantly down the sides of the cake, but not to run straight off. Add a little more icing sugar or water if necessary.

Turn the cool cake(s) out of their tins and remove the baking paper. Drizzle over the icing, allowing it to trickle down the sides of the cakes. A little tip to save your wire rack from getting covered in sticky icing and to save you some washing up: just turn the loaf tin(s) upside down, sit the cake(s) on top of those, and ice them there.

Allow the icing to set slightly before you slice and serve – this is brilliant with fresh raspberries.

PECAN PIE

This is the New World cousin of the very British treacle tart. In the States, where pecans are a native nut, this more luxurious version was born. Originally we'd planned on baking these just twice a year, at Thanksgiving and on 4th July, but we caved into demand from customers, and now sell them all year round.

METHOD

Prepare and bake the tart case.

To make the filling, stir together the golden syrup, muscovado sugar, butter and milk in a small saucepan over a medium heat. As soon as everything has melted and come together into a smooth sauce, set the pan aside to cool slightly.

Beat the eggs in a small mixing bowl. Gradually pour the warm syrup onto the eggs in a steady stream, whisking as you go. Stir through the chopped pecans, then pour the mixture into the tart case. Bake for 20 minutes, or until the filling has set and the nuts are bound together.

While the tart cools slightly, warm the honey very gently in a small pan over a low heat. You want it to become smooth and liquid, but not to boil. Use a soft pastry brush to glaze the top of the tart with the runny honey.

VARIATIONS: To make a tipsier tart, add a few tablespoons of dark rum, bourbon or even Frangelico to the mixture in place of the milk.

INGREDIENTS

For the tart case:
1 x 24cm baked sweet almond
   tart case (see p.33 for the
   pastry and p.31 for how to
   blind-bake)

For the filling:
120g golden syrup
120g light muscovado sugar
40g butter
1 tbsp milk
2 eggs
230g pecans, toasted (see p.35)
   and roughly chopped

For the topping:
3 tbsp clear honey

Serves: 8

APPLE CRUMBLE CAKE

Apple cake is particularly associated with Rosh Hashanah, the Jewish New Year, when dishes made with apples or honey take centre stage – these ingredients symbolise the sweetness hoped for in the coming year. It will fill your house with wonderful smells that wrap around you like a comforting blanket. It's so packed with apple that it's almost more fruit held together with cake than it is cake with fruit in it, while using oil means it keeps far longer than butter-based cakes.

METHOD

Butter two loaf tins about 19cm x 8cm, or one large loaf tin measuring 24cm x 10cm, then line with baking paper. Preheat the oven to 200°C/gas mark 6. Sift together the flour, salt, spices and bicarbonate of soda and set aside.

In a stand mixer fitted with the beater, beat the eggs on a low speed, then gradually add the sugar, beating all the time. Once all the sugar has been added, pour in the oil in a slow, constant stream and beat until you have a very thick, pale mixture – you're creating an emulsion. Stop the mixer, add the flour mixture all in one go, and mix again very briefly until just combined. Add the apples and fold them in with a large metal spoon until the fruit is stirred right through. Spoon it into the cake tin or tins, smooth the top, then sprinkle the tops with crumble. Place in the oven and immediately reduce the temperature to 170°C/gas mark 3. Bake the cakes for 40–45 minutes (for two small cakes) or 1 hour–1 hour 10 minutes for a large cake. They are ready when risen, springy and when a skewer inserted into the centre(s) comes out clean. Leave in the tin until completely cool.

This cake is so moist that it will keep for 3–4 days without trouble. Store it on a wooden board, loosely covered with a cloth, rather than in an airtight container.

INGREDIENTS

2 eggs, at room temperature
180g caster sugar
220ml vegetable oil
200g plain flour
1 tsp ground cinnamon
1 tsp mixed spice
½ tsp ground cloves
½ tsp grated nutmeg
1 tsp bicarbonate of soda
½ tsp fine sea salt
300g peeled, cored Bramley apples (roughly 3 apples), cut into 1cm cubes
½ quantity crumble topping (see p.32)

Makes: 1 large or 2 small loaf cakes

CARROT CAKE

This recipe dates back to our very first bakery in Hampstead, and is one of the many amazing creations of Kit Williams, a star baker who has worked with us right from the start. This is by far our most popular cake and we just can't make enough: they sell out far more quickly than we can bake them. You won't be able to identify the flavour of the pineapple here, but it's a secret ingredient that adds even more moisture and introduces a welcome, slightly tart edge. It's far easier to ice this cake neatly if you bake it the day before and refrigerate it overnight.

METHOD

Preheat the oven to 170°C/gas mark 3. Butter 2 x 22cm round sandwich tins and line their bases with a circle of non-stick baking paper.

Whisk the eggs and sugar together in the bowl of a stand mixer, or using a hand mixer, until thick and pale yellow. With the machine running, add the oil in a steady stream. Finally, whisk in the vanilla.

In a separate bowl, sift together the flour, baking powder, bicarbonate of soda, cinnamon and salt. Use a large metal spoon to fold these by hand into the egg mixture. Finally, stir in the carrots, pineapple and pecans until completely combined. Divide the batter equally between both cake tins and smooth the surfaces. Bake for 40–45 minutes until risen and springy to the touch and a skewer pushed into their centres comes out clean. Leave to cool on a wire rack before turning out. Ideally, chill overnight, well-wrapped in cling film.

Make the icing using an electric mixer. If your cream cheese and butter aren't both at room temperature, your icing will separate and turn grainy. With the beater fitted, beat the butter until virtually white, fluffy, creamy and shiny. This will take at least 5 minutes at high speed. Stop the mixer, scrape down the sides and the beater, add the icing sugar and beat for another 3–4 minutes, starting at low speed and increasing to high. Beat the cream cheese with a wooden spoon or spatula until it has the same consistency as the butter icing, then mix in at a low speed. If you see any lumps, stop the mixer and use a rubber spatula to finish things off.

To assemble, take the cakes out of the fridge and place one on a serving plate. With a palette knife, spread a quarter of the icing onto it, then top with the second cake. Use just enough icing to coat the top and sides of the cake with a very thin layer, capturing all the crumbs that might otherwise spoil your icing – this is called the 'crumb coat', for obvious reasons. Put into the freezer for 5 minutes, or the fridge for 20–30 minutes, until the crumb coat has set. Spread the remaining icing all over the top and sides in a smooth, even layer. Chill in the fridge until the icing is set – around 30 minutes.

INGREDIENTS

For the cake:
4 eggs
360g caster sugar
225ml rapeseed or other neutral-flavoured vegetable oil
2 tsp natural vanilla extract
300g plain flour
2 tsp baking powder
2 tsp bicarbonate of soda
1 tsp ground cinnamon
½ tsp fine sea salt
480g carrots, peeled and grated (about 5 carrots)
180g pineapple, chopped into little chunks (save and include all the juice that runs off as you chop it)
90g pecans, toasted and roughly chopped (see p.35 for how to toast nuts)

For the cream cheese icing:
200g butter, at room temperature
150g icing sugar
500g full-fat white soft cheese, at room temperature

Serves: 8

FLOURLESS CHOCOLATE CAKE

This cake packs as much chocolate per square centimetre as possible, and then some. Its texture is as light as its flavour is rich, since the technique involves making and then baking what is basically a chocolate mousse. As if you weren't sold on it already, it's also gluten-free.

We bake this in two stages to create an oozing, gooey, self-saucing top layer. You can prepare the first stage a day in advance, if you like.

METHOD

Butter a 20cm springform cake tin. Line the base with non-stick baking paper, then butter this, too. Preheat the oven to 170°C/gas mark 3.

Melt the butter and chocolate in a small heatproof dish fitted snugly over a small saucepan of gently simmering water, making sure that its base doesn't actually touch the water. Stir to combine. Remove the bowl from the pan and beat in the cocoa powder. Pour into a very large mixing bowl and set aside to cool slightly, but not to room temperature.

In the bowl of a stand mixer, or using a hand mixer, whisk the egg yolks with 100g of the caster sugar plus all the muscovado sugar at high speed, until the mixture grows to three times its original volume and becomes very pale and thick. This will take 8–10 minutes.

Now to whisk the egg whites: if using a stand mixer, carefully empty the yolks and sugar mixture into a clean bowl, then wash and dry the mixer bowl thoroughly before adding the egg whites. If using a hand mixer, place the egg whites in a clean bowl. Either way, make sure that not a speck or grease or dirt remains in the bowl, or the egg whites won't whip up. A useful tip here – wipe the inside of the bowl with a few drops of lemon juice and some kitchen paper. This eliminates any fat or oil that could cause you problems.

Whisk the egg whites with the salt until the mixture doubles in size and holds soft peaks. Slowly begin to add the remaining 50g of caster sugar as you whisk, a tablespoonful at a time. Once added, continue to whisk until the mixture holds soft peaks, and has the consistency of whipped cream.

INGREDIENTS

240g butter, at room temperature, diced
240g dark chocolate (at least 70 per cent cocoa), chopped into rough chunks
85g cocoa powder
8 eggs, separated
150g caster sugar
100g light muscovado sugar
½ tsp fine sea salt
cocoa powder, for dusting
crème fraîche, to serve (optional)

Serves: 8

You now have three components: the still-warm chocolate mixture, the yolk mixture, and the whisked whites. Add a big spoonful of yolk mixture to the chocolate and whisk in well to loosen it a little, then add the rest of the yolks and fold in gently. Take a third of the whites on a large metal spoon and fold into the chocolate mixture to loosen it, then carefully fold in the next third, then the final one. Don't over-mix – the odd streak of white is preferable to knocking out all the air you've taken so much time to whisk in.

Pour two-thirds of the batter gently into the prepared tin, holding the bowl close to the tin so that it doesn't have far to fall – this would only knock out the air. Cover the remaining third of the batter tightly with cling film and set aside. Don't level out the batter in the tin – allow it to spread of its own accord. Bake the cake for 35–40 minutes. The edges should form a slight crust, while the middle should still be a little wobbly. Remove from the oven, allow to cool completely, then cover the tin with cling film and chill for at least 1 hour or overnight.

When you're ready for the second stage of baking, preheat the oven to 200°C/gas mark 6. Spread the reserved batter on top of the chilled cake as you would spread icing, building it up slightly more thickly towards the centre. Bake for 10 minutes, until this fresh layer of cake has set. A thin skin should form on top, but it should still feel runny underneath. As soon as it turns from shiny to matt, it's ready. Leave to cool, then run a knife around the edge to make sure the cake isn't sticking to the sides.

When completely cool, unmould and dust thickly with cocoa powder. Serve in very thin slices – this is gloriously rich – perhaps with dollops of crème fraîche. The top layer should be soft, almost a chocolate sauce, while the bottom layer will be firmer. To get the full effect, serve this the day you make it. The contrast between the two layers won't be as noticeable if you leave it longer, though it will still be absolutely delicious. (See p.203 for photograph.)

BLACKBERRY AND APPLE TRAY BAKE

This is a dead easy tray-bake. Served warm, it makes for the perfect autumn dessert, accompanied by cream, custard or thick yoghurt, plus extra fresh berries or compôte. Keep the fruit seasonal and mix it up to suit your tastes – summer berries, peach and blueberry, rhubarb and strawberry, pear and stem ginger. If you find the fruit you choose has a tendency to sink to the bottom as the cake cooks, next time, toss it very lightly in flour and shake off any excess in a sieve or colander before stirring into the batter.

METHOD

Preheat the oven to 170°C/gas mark 3. Butter and flour a deep pudding dish about 20cm x 30cm. Toss the slices of apples in the lemon juice to prevent them from browning.

Pour the cream into a saucepan, add the butter, and place over a medium heat. Allow the butter to melt, stirring, but don't let it come to the boil. Remove from the heat and allow to cool slightly.

Beat the eggs with the sugar in a bowl until well combined, then pour on the warm cream mixture, stirring all the time. Fold in the flour with a large metal spoon, then stir through the berries and slices of apple. Pour everything into the baking dish. Bake for about 40 minutes, by which point it should be puffed up, lightly golden and very slightly crisp at the edges. A skewer pushed into the centre should come out clean – take care not to over-bake this or it will lose its lightness.

INGREDIENTS

175g butter, plus extra
   for greasing
300g plain flour, plus extra
   for dusting
1 small Bramley apple, cored,
   peeled, quartered and
   thinly sliced
2 small red apples, cored
   and thinly sliced
2 tbsp lemon juice
300ml double cream
3 eggs
220g caster sugar
1 tsp vanilla extract
300g fresh blackberries

Serves: 6–8

BAKED VANILLA AND WHITE CHOCOLATE CHEESECAKE

This is an American-style cheesecake – luscious, rich, creamy and smooth. Instead of the usual crushed digestive biscuit base, we make our own biscuit: it's designed to mimic the flavour of the classic American Graham cracker base, which is the best possible foil for the cheesecake above. If you want to save time, you can use 250g shop-bought biscuits: ginger nuts would be particularly good.

This is best made the day before serving, and will take over your oven for hours, so make sure you don't need it for anything else in the meantime.

METHOD

Preheat the oven to 180°C/gas mark 4 and line a baking sheet with non-stick baking paper. Butter a 20cm springform cake tin and line it with baking paper too.

Begin by making the base. Whisk together the flour, muscovado sugar, bicarbonate of soda and salt in a large bowl, then scatter over the cold cubes of butter and use your fingertips to rub it into the dry ingredients until the mixture resembles coarse breadcrumbs. In a separate bowl, stir together the honey, vanilla and milk. Pour this into the flour mix and stir vigorously until you're left with a soft, paste-like dough.

Press the dough out onto the lined baking sheet to a thickness of about 5mm and bake for 20–25 minutes, until cooked through but still a little soft. Leave to cool completely – it will crisp up as it cools. Break it up and crush it into crumbs: either use a food processor or put the biscuit in a plastic bag and bash it with a rolling pin (very therapeutic). Tip the crumbs into a bowl, pour over the melted butter and stir until you have a damp, sandy mixture, then press this down evenly into the base of the cake tin and freeze while you make the filling.

Reduce the oven temperature to 160°C/gas mark 3. For the filling, pour the double cream into a small pan over a medium heat. Bring it gently to the boil, remove from the heat, then add the chopped white chocolate. Stir occasionally as the chocolate melts into the cream, then set aside to cool to room temperature.

Meanwhile, tip the cream cheese into the bowl of a stand mixer fitted with the beater, or use a handmixer and a large bowl. Beat on a medium speed until completely smooth. Add the caster sugar and carry on mixing.

Continued overleaf

INGREDIENTS

For the base:
100g plain flour
60g light muscovado sugar
½ tsp bicarbonate of soda
½ tsp fine sea salt
35g butter, chilled and diced,
    plus extra for greasing
35g clear honey
2 tsp natural vanilla extract
2 tbsp milk
100g butter, melted

For the filling:
180ml double cream
200g white chocolate,
    chopped into rough chunks
500g full-fat white soft cheese,
    at room temperature
100g caster sugar
4 eggs, at room temperature
1 vanilla pod

For the topping:
35g icing sugar, sifted
200ml sour cream
fresh raspberries or blueberries,
    to decorate (optional)

Serves: 8

In a separate bowl, beat the eggs with a whisk. Use a sharp knife to split open the vanilla pod and scrape out the seeds, then whisk these into the eggs. Pour the eggs slowly into the cream cheese, beating constantly as you go. Take your time to prevent the mixture from curdling. When everything is combined, reduce the speed to slow. Now add the white chocolate cream and mix until you have a silky batter.

Pour the filling into the cake tin, on top of the base, and bake for 1½ hours. The cake should stay very white. If you see it starting to brown, reduce the oven to 150°C. While the cheesecake cooks, prepare the topping. Whisk the icing sugar into the sour cream until completely smooth, then cover and chill until needed.

Remove the cheesecake from the oven and let it sit for 10 minutes to cool in its tin. Gently, taking care not to break through the top of the cheesecake, spread the topping in a neat circle in the centre with the back of a spoon, leaving a 2cm border around the edge. Put back into the oven for 10 minutes more. It's ready when still a little wobbly at the centre, and a pale white – don't allow it to colour. At this stage, switch off the oven and open the door slightly. Leave the cheesecake to sit there for at least 2 hours, cooling slowly. The more slowly it cools, the less it will crack. Cracks aren't disastrous – a cracked cheesecake is still a delicious cheesecake – but a smooth, crevice-free top is even better. When the cheesecake reaches room temperature, cover it with cling film and chill it overnight to get nice and firm, before unmoulding and serving. For an even more impressive dessert, pile fresh raspberries or blueberries on top.

SUPPER

PIZZETTE BIANCA

Or 'little white pizzas': white, because they don't include the tomato sauce we've almost come to expect on pizzas and little, because we like to make individual portions rather than one large pizza – easier to bake, easier to serve, and easier to make sure everyone gets their fair share of toppings. The instant we tested these at GAIL's Kitchen we knew they had to go right on the menu. They've been among our bestselling dishes (though we vary the toppings with the seasons) ever since. It's basically a way to show off some of Italy's finest produce by sitting it atop one of our favourite doughs. Because you only bake the base, it's almost like a salad on a flatbread.

Burrata is a super fresh Italian cheese. A mozzarella shell filled with mozzarella and cream. And it is every bit as luscious as that sounds. Burratina are small balls of burrata. If you can't find these, then use the freshest mozzarella you can find. If you were to try to use one large burrata, the creamy, liquid centre would be lost as you divided it up. (See photograph overleaf.)

METHOD

Begin by preparing the artichokes. Strip the outer leaves away to reveal the hearts, leaving the stems attached, taking care to pare away the hairy chokes to leave only the edible cores. Sit the hearts in a small pan and pour over the olive oil to cover them – how much you need will depend on the size of your artichokes. Add the lemon zest, lemon juice, garlic, bay leaf and white wine. Set the pan over a very gentle heat and warm it through, but don't let it boil at any point – you shouldn't see any bubbles at all. You may need to increase and decrease the heat at intervals to achieve this balance. Cook until the hearts are soft when pierced with a knife – between 10 and 20 minutes, depending on how fresh the artichokes are. Remove from the heat, leave them to cool completely in the perfumed oil, and then remove with a slotted spoon and cut into small wedges. Whatever you do, don't discard the cooking oil, which is now infused with flavour – save it for cooking with, for dressing salads or just for dunking bread.

To make the crumb topping, preheat the oven to 170°C/gas mark 3 and line a baking sheet with non-stick baking paper. Blitz the bread roughly in a blender or food processor until you have coarse crumbs. Spread the crumbs out evenly on the baking sheet, and bake for 15 minutes until golden and crunchy. Move them around halfway through the cooking time to ensure they toast evenly. You want them very dry so they can absorb plenty of flavour later on. Set aside to cool completely, then, in a large bowl, toss them with the thyme and oregano leaves, lemon juice and zest, chopped black olives, crushed garlic, red wine vinegar, and salt and pepper to taste. Add just enough olive oil to moisten the whole mixture, but no more than the breadcrumbs can easily absorb.

INGREDIENTS

For the pizzette bases:
½ quantity focaccia dough
    after the final rising
    (see p.57)
olive oil, for greasing and
    brushing
flaked sea salt, for sprinkling

For the artichokes:
8 violet artichokes
300–500ml olive oil
1 strip of lemon zest
½ lemon (juice only)
2 garlic cloves, lightly crushed
1 bay leaf
125ml dry white wine

To make the bases, increase the oven temperature to 220°C/gas mark 7 and lightly oil two baking sheets, using your hands so that your hands are oily too.

Take the dough and divide it into 8 portions (each will weigh about 60g). Form them into rough balls and push them out into rough little pizza shapes about 20cm across. Don't obsess over creating perfect round pizzas – amoeba-shapes are fine. Use your fingers to stretch and play with the dough. It will shrink back as you shape it, so give it time to relax. You don't want make the pizzette too thin or too even, or you'll lose the fluffy, almost melt-in-your mouth feel that the slightly thicker parts will have. The surface of the pizzette should be very slightly oiled, just from where you've been touching them with your oiled hands.

Put them on the baking sheets and leave for 20–30 minutes at room temperature, uncovered, to relax. Bake for 12–15 minutes, until puffed, risen and lightly golden, but not stiff or crunchy. Remove from the oven, quickly brush lightly with olive oil and sprinkle with a little flaked sea salt.

To assemble, arrange the cheese on top – either the individual balls of burrata, or hand-torn pieces of mozzarella. Follow with the artichoke wedges, then folded-over slices of ham, and a sprinkling of garlicky breadcrumbs to finish.

For the crumb topping:

120g sourdough bread, crusts removed (weight without crusts)
10 sprigs of thyme, leaves only
5 sprigs of young oregano, leaves only
½ lemon (juice only)
40g stoned black olives, roughly chopped
1 garlic clove, crushed
2 tsp red wine vinegar
flaked sea salt and freshly ground black pepper
olive oil

To finish:

250g burratina, or super-fresh mozzarella
16 slices of Parma ham, cut thinner than paper

Makes: 8 pizzettes

LEEKS VINAIGRETTE WITH MAPLE AND MUSTARD CROUTONS

Here's a springtime starter, perfect in its simplicity, and a wonderful way of serving young leeks. Swap the leeks for all kinds of delicate vegetables – asparagus, green beans or, even, grilled (rather than poached) spring onions.

Baby leeks vary in size from the width of your little finger to that of your thumb, so use your judgement when deciding how many each person is likely to eat.

METHOD

Begin by poaching the leeks for 3 minutes in a pan of briskly simmering, well-salted water. You want to break down the fibres to leave them silky and soft, but still intact. Drain them and leave to cool.

Lower the eggs into gently simmering water and boil for 6 minutes. You're aiming for yolks that are completely solid, but still a vibrant primrose yellow. Immediately lift them out of the pan with a slotted spoon, tap them firmly with the back of a spoon to just crack the shells, then place in a bowl of cold water until cooled. Peel carefully and set aside.

Preheat the oven to 170°C/gas mark 3 and line a baking sheet with baking paper. Toss the chunks of bread with the mustard and the maple syrup, then mix in the salt, pepper and thyme leaves. Spread evenly on the baking sheet and toast in the oven for 15–20 minutes until golden and crunchy, stirring halfway through to ensure an even cooking. The maple syrup will mean that the bread turns rather dark, but don't worry – the important thing is that it's crisped right through.

Make the vinaigrette: with a hand whisk, blend together the egg yolk, mustard and white wine vinegar. Whisk in the olive oil all in one go, then taste and season with sea salt and pepper. If it's too acidic, add a pinch (or two) of sugar, or, if you want it fresher and brighter, squeeze in a little of the lemon juice. When the balance of flavours is spot on, continue whisking and trickle in the rapeseed oil in a slow, steady stream, so that an emulsion forms. You're aiming for a very thick dressing, almost the consistency of runny mayonnaise.

Lay the leeks on a platter or divide between individual serving plates. Spoon a few teaspoons of vinaigrette over each portion. With a coarse grater, grate one egg each over each plate, then sprinkle the crunchy bread on top. Drizzle lightly with a little extra olive oil to serve.

INGREDIENTS

For the leeks:
20–30 baby leeks, depending on how thick they are, cleaned and left whole
4 eggs, at room temperature

For the maple and mustard croutons:
100g sourdough bread, without crusts, torn roughly into 1–2cm chunks
1 tbsp Dijon mustard
1 tbsp maple syrup
1 tsp flaked sea salt
½ tsp freshly ground black pepper
5 sprigs of thyme, leaves only
olive oil, for drizzling

For the vinaigrette:
1 egg yolk
1 tbsp Dijon mustard
1 tbsp white wine vinegar
3 tbsp olive oil, plus extra for drizzling
pinch of caster sugar
½ lemon (juice only)
3 tbsp rapeseed oil

Serves: 4 as a starter or side

BAKED SARDINES WITH SOURDOUGH CRUMBS AND HERITAGE TOMATO SALAD

Some dishes taste better outdoors, and this is one of them – the perfect light summer supper for an evening in the garden.

This recipe is a homage to the cooking of one woman in Roy's home town, Tel Aviv. She runs a restaurant – though it's so simple it barely merits the name – on the beach. She opens when she feels like it and closes when she doesn't and, despite the stripped-back surroundings, everything she touches in her kitchen turns to gold. Her sardine sandwiches are works of art, and they're what Roy had in mind when creating this recipe.

The oily fish works brilliantly with the sweet acidity of the tomatoes and the sea-saltiness of the anchovies and capers. Sardines and tomatoes are at their best at the same time of year and together their flavours sing of the south and the Mediterranean.

Make your life easier by asking your fishmonger to clean and butterfly the sardines for you.

METHOD

Remove any visible bones left in the butterflied sardines and set aside. Now make the sourdough breadcrumbs. Preheat the oven to 170°C/gas mark 3 and line a baking sheet with non-stick baking paper. Blitz the bread roughly in a blender or food processor until you have coarse crumbs. Spread them out evenly on the baking sheet, and bake for 15 minutes until golden and crunchy. Move them around halfway through the cooking time to ensure they toast evenly. You want them very dry so they can absorb plenty of flavour later on. Set aside once ready and leave to cool.

Meanwhile, in a large bowl, soak the currants in the sherry vinegar for 10–15 minutes, until they've absorbed most of the liquid. Add 1 tablespoon of the olive oil to a pan over a low heat, and heat the shallot and the garlic very gently. You want to warm them in the oil, but not to cook or soften them.

Continued overleaf

INGREDIENTS

8 sardines, cleaned and
   butterflied

For the sourdough salsa:
2–3 thick slices of day-old
   sourdough bread (about 150g
   once the crusts are removed)
25g currants
1 tbsp sherry vinegar, plus
   extra for drizzling
4 tbsp olive oil, plus extra for
   cooking and drizzling
1 small shallot, finely chopped
1 garlic clove, crushed
2 tbsp Lilliput capers, in brine,
   drained
4 sprigs of mint, leaves only,
   roughly chopped
1 lemon (finely grated zest)
4 fillets of anchovies
   preserved in oil, drained
   and roughly chopped
½ tsp flaked sea salt
½ tsp dried chilli flakes
25g pine nuts, toasted
   (see p.35)

For the tomato salad:
about 12 small heritage (or
   2 large) tomatoes per
   person – a mix of colours
   and shapes
4 sprigs of oregano,
   leaves only
4 sprigs of mint, leaves only
flaked sea salt and freshly
   ground black pepper,
   to taste

Serves: 4

In the large bowl combine the toasted breadcrumbs, the currants (and any vinegar that they didn't soak up), capers, chopped mint, lemon zest, anchovies, salt and chilli flakes. Mix well, then add the warm shallots and garlic, the pine nuts and all the remaining olive oil. Stir until you have a wet, crunchy mixture. Cover and leave for up to 2 hours for the flavours to meld – no longer, or the mixture will become too soggy.

To prepare the salad, slice the tomatoes in as many different ways as you can, creating a real mix of shapes, textures and colours – halve some, roughly chop others, slice a few thinly. If what you have looks beautiful now, it will look even more so on the plate. Add the oregano and mint, drizzle with a little olive oil, and add a few drops of vinegar, and salt and pepper to taste.

Cook the fish: preheat the oven to 220°C/gas mark 7 and line a baking sheet with non-stick baking paper. Heat 1 tablespoon of olive oil in a large frying pan over a medium heat. In two batches, if necessary, lay the sardine fillets in the frying pan, skin-side down, and cook for a maximum of 3 minutes. The edges of the fish will begin to turn white, while the centre will still be uncooked – don't worry, they'll cook through thoroughly in the oven.

When the fish have been seared in the pan, transfer them to the prepared baking sheet, skin-side up, and cover with half of the sourdough salsa. Pop into the oven to warm through for 2–3 minutes, then leave to rest for 5 minutes.

Arrange the tomato salad either on individual plates or on a large platter. Lay the sardines on top of the tomatoes, piling and layering them slightly over each other, and sprinkle over the remaining sourdough salsa.

SPRING VEGETABLE STEW ON TOAST WITH GOAT'S CURD

Quite rightly, it's often emphasised how little cooking young spring vegetables need. For the most part, we tend to cook them as briefly as possible. But in this recipe we take the opposite tack, and slow-cook them in a rich, savoury broth. It makes for a totally different experience. This springtime stew is inspired by the Italian dish, Vignole. It calls for the softest, youngest goat's cheese you can find, which is in season at the same time of year. Goat's curd still has that distinctive tang that all products made from goat's milk possess, but in the mildest possible form. You could even use goat's milk yoghurt, which is now widely available – just strain it in a cloth overnight to remove the excess moisture, and to concentrate all the flavour. You'll have something not far from a soft, spreadable cheese. If you struggle to find either, ricotta will also work well, but add a pinch of salt. If you want to make this vegetarian, leave out the pancetta and use vegetable stock.

METHOD

Strip the outer leaves from the artichokes to reveal their hearts, and pare and trim away all the hairy chokes. Chop the hearts into 6 pieces.

Heat a generous dash of olive oil in a large frying pan over a medium heat. Fry the onion with the pancetta until the onion is soft – 8–10 minutes. Add the crushed garlic and cook for another 1–2 minutes, until fragrant, but not coloured. Pour in 150ml of the stock – you may need more later, depending on how dry the stew becomes while cooking. (You're aiming for a good amount of liquid, but not quite a soup, so add more stock as and when required.) Add the artichoke hearts and the stems and ribs of the chard, bring to the boil, then simmer for 10 minutes, stirring occasionally. Add the broad beans and peas and cook for another 10 minutes, then stir in the chard leaves and cook for a further 10 minutes. Add the mint, season with salt and pepper, and squeeze in the lemon juice. Finish with a generous glug of olive oil.

Meanwhile, brush the slices of sourdough on each side with olive oil and sprinkle with a little salt. Grill on both sides until almost charred, but still soft within. Smear one side with a generous layer of goat's curd. Sit each toast in the centre of a shallow bowl and spoon a generous pile of stew onto half of the bread, letting the broth cover the base of the bowl, with the bright white of the curd shining through on the other half.

INGREDIENTS

For the stew:
6 small violet artichokes – smaller than a tennis ball
olive oil, for frying, grilling and to finish
1 red onion, chopped
100g diced pancetta or lardons
2 garlic cloves, crushed
200ml chicken stock
a bunch of Swiss chard, washed, dried and chopped to separate the stems and thick ribs from the leafy parts
200g shelled broad beans
250g fresh shelled peas – or frozen, at a push
5 sprigs of mint, leaves only, chopped
flaked sea salt and freshly ground black pepper, to taste
good squeeze of lemon juice

For the toasts:
4 thick slices of sourdough bread
200g goat's curd, or other soft cheese

Serves: 4

STONEGROUND POLENTA CHIPS

These polenta chips are more of a nibble or a snack and are excellent with beer – or a very dry martini. They are crispy and chewy at the same time. If you're watching a film, settling in for an afternoon of sport on the TV, or having people over for drinks, they're just the ticket.

You need stoneground yellow polenta for this recipe, and not the instant kind. Polenta isn't an ingredient that's big on flavour in its own right – it's more of a way to let other flavours shine. If you do want to add extra punch to the chips themselves, you can stir in more butter or olive oil, extra cheese, or some cayenne. Whatever you do, don't be shy with the salt. Make the day before, as they need to chill overnight. See over the page for topping ideas.

METHOD

Mix the polenta and water together in a large pan, bring slowly to the boil. Reduce the heat and simmer for 40 minutes, stirring regularly, until the mixture resembles overcooked porridge, pulls away from the edges of the pan as you stir (which will be hard work), and the bubbles pop up loudly and alarmingly through the viscous mixture. Add the garlic, Parmesan, butter and plenty of salt – more than you might think. It's difficult to judge the seasoning accurately when the polenta is still hot, so let a small spoonful cool for a few seconds on a plate before checking the flavour and adding more salt or butter as you see fit.

Line a large loaf tin with non-stick baking paper. Pour in the polenta, level the top, wrap well with cling film, and leave to cool to room temperature. Chill overnight, until completely firm and not unlike a rubber brick.

Turn out the block of polenta. Cut it in half lengthwise. With a very sharp knife, slice each half widthwise into 5mm slices. Keep each piece nice and thin to get the gorgeous crisp texture you're after.

Half-fill a large pan with oil, for deep frying, and heat it to 180°C or until a cube of bread browns in 30 seconds. Deep-fry the chips in batches until lightly golden and crisp – about 3 minutes. Remove with a slotted spoon, and drain on kitchen paper. Sprinkle with extra salt as they cool.

INGREDIENTS

200g stoneground polenta
800ml water
1 garlic clove, crushed
70g Parmesan, finely grated
good knob of butter
flaked sea salt, to taste
vegetable oil, for deep-frying

Serves: 6

BURNT TOMATO DIP

These have a light fragrant flavour, perfect to nibble with cool, long drinks on a summer's evening. The tomatoes and onions are even better roasted over charcoal, rather than in the oven, but unless you're already planning a barbecue, that's not really practical!

METHOD

Preheat the oven to 220°C/gas mark 7 and line a baking sheet with baking paper. Mix the tomatoes and onion wedges in a large bowl and pour over a generous amount of olive oil, tossing to coat them well. Season generously with salt, then spread on the baking sheet.

Roast the tomatoes for 15–20 minutes until they start to blacken and char slightly. Don't be afraid to really get a good burnt skin on the outside of the vegetables – this is what will give the smoky flavour you're after.

Once ready, set aside to cool, then blitz in a food processor with a little more olive oil – about 2 tablespoons – the lemon juice, and a little more salt and pepper to taste, plus the ground coriander, if using. Pulse until you're left with a rather chunky sauce – don't liquidise. Taste, and, if it's a little too acidic, add a pinch of sugar. Serve in a small bowl along with another bowl of sour cream and a pile of the polenta chips for dipping and dunking.

INGREDIENTS

4 ripe, juicy tomatoes, halved
1 red onion, cut into 6 wedges
olive oil, for roasting and
    drizzling
flaked sea salt and freshly
    ground black pepper, to taste
½ lemon (juice only)
1 tsp coriander seeds, toasted
    and ground to a powder
    (optional but good)
pinch of sugar (optional)
1 small pot of sour cream

Serves: 6

GORGONZOLA DOLCE DRESSING

We love this when the weather is cold and uninviting and you need something warm and comforting to nibble.

METHOD

Bring the double cream to the boil in a small pan, then remove from the heat and drop in the cheese, a lump at a time, whisking until smooth. Taste, and see if it needs a little salt – this will depend on how sweet your cheese was to begin with.

Leave to cool and thicken slightly for a minute or two, then drizzle over a pile of polenta chips and let everyone dig in.

INGREDIENTS

100ml double cream
100g sweet Gorgonzola, diced
flaked sea salt, to taste

Serves: 6

STUFFED CHICKEN

Like everything we do, this recipe is literally centred around wheat – albeit bulgur wheat, a slightly different form to the kind that goes into our bread. Bulgur comes in different varieties, from coarse to finely ground. You need the coarse kind for this recipe.

This is practically a meal in itself, all wrapped up in savoury little parcels, but quicker and easier than roasting a whole bird. A salad or some very lightly cooked greens are all it needs.

METHOD

Preheat the oven to 200°C/gas mark 6. Prepare the bulgur according to packet directions. Set aside.

To make the stuffing, heat the oil over a medium heat in a frying pan. Add the onions and the pine nuts and cook for 8–10 minutes, stirring regularly, until the onion has softened.

Stir the parsley, lemon zest and juice, curry powder, cumin, cooked onions and pine nuts into the cooked bulgur wheat and season with salt and pepper to taste.

Open out the boned chicken thighs and fill with the stuffing, using it all up. Roll them back together, then pack them tightly together in a small roasting tin, so that they don't come unrolled. Bake for 30 minutes, until the chicken is cooked through, and the stuffing is moist.

INGREDIENTS

100g coarse bulgur wheat
50ml olive oil
2 onions, finely chopped
20g pine nuts, toasted (see p.35)
small bunch of parsley, leaves
    only, roughly chopped
1–2 lemons, depending on
    size and juiciness (finely
    grated zest and juice)
1 tsp mild curry powder
½ tsp ground cumin
flaked sea salt and freshly
    ground black pepper, to taste
8 boned chicken thighs, skin
    left on (or ask the butcher
    to bone them for you)

Serves: 4

RED MULLET ON TOAST

This was of the first recipes that Jonathan cooked for us when he joined the team at GAIL's Kitchen. We were blown away: he's now our Head Chef, so it must have been good. When you go to the fishmongers, choose your mullet according to how you want to serve this. For a starter buy smaller fish; for a main dish, pick bigger ones. The fishmonger will fillet them for you if necessary.

METHOD

First, make the sauce. Chop the roasted peppers then place in a pan with the remaining sauce ingredients. Bring to the boil over a medium heat. Reduce the heat, part-cover and simmer incredibly gently for 2–2½ hours, until the sauce is reduced and jam-like – thick, dark and richly flavoured. Taste and add more salt, pepper or sugar if you think it's necessary, then set aside.

Roughly chop the greens – if they have thick, slightly tough stems, separate these from the leaves and blanch for 5 minutes in boiling, salted water until tender, then drain. Drizzle a little olive oil in the base of a large pan over a medium heat. Wash the chopped greens and drain but leave a little water clinging to the leaves. Tip them into the pan and cover it for 30 seconds, then remove the lid, stir, and season with the salt and pepper. Wait until all the leaves are just beginning to wilt, then immediately remove from the heat. They should have reduced in volume by roughly half.

Brush the slices of sourdough on both sides with olive oil and sprinkle with a little salt. Grill on each side until slightly charred at the edges, but still soft within.

Preheat the oven to 200°C/gas mark 6. Sit the toasts on a baking sheet and top with the wilted greens. Divide the tomato sauce amongst them, then sit the fillets of fish on top. Drizzle with a little more oil and season with salt and pepper. Bake for 15 minutes, until the mullet is cooked through – the exact time will depend on the size of your fish.

TO MAKE IN ADVANCE: The tomato sauce can be made up to 3 days before and stored in the fridge.

INGREDIENTS

2 large red mullet, each
    filleted into two fillets

For the tomato and
    pepper sauce:
2 red peppers, roasted
    and peeled (see p.160)
400g can chopped tomatoes
225ml rapeseed oil
1 garlic bulb, all the cloves
    peeled and thinly sliced
4 celery sticks, the outsides
    shaved with a vegetable
    peeler to strip off the fibrous
    strings, roughly chopped
1 small red chilli, seeds
    removed and chopped
1 tsp sweet paprika
pinch of caster sugar, to taste
flaked sea salt and freshly
    ground black pepper,
    to taste

For the base:
large bunch of Swiss or
    rainbow chard, or spinach
olive oil, for cooking
    and brushing
8 thick slices of sourdough
    bread
flaked sea salt and freshly
    ground black pepper,
    to taste

Serves: 4

SUMMER PUDDING

The ripest seasonal berries need very little help from the cook: they're a treat in themselves. A classic English summer pudding highlights their flavour with a bare minimum of cooking, and is a time-honoured way to use up leftover bread. Our version uses leftover croissants: slightly dry croissants are fantastically absorbent – even more so than bread – and soak up the fruit's deep purple, wine-coloured juices to perfection. That said, you could always substitute any white bread with the crusts cut off.

METHOD

Wash the blackcurrants, redcurrants and raspberries and pick them over to remove any stems or leaves. Place in a large mixing bowl. Add the sugar to the berries and toss well. Cover, and leave to macerate for 5– 6 hours at room temperature, or overnight in the fridge. When you take them out, you'll have rather sad-looking, collapsed berries, and plenty of rich, purple sauce.

Tip them into a large pan and add the water, then taste for sweetness. If the mixture is very tangy, you can add a little more sugar. Split open the vanilla pod with a sharp knife, scrape out the seeds, then add these to the pan along with the pod. Gently bring the berries to a boil, then increase the heat and boil for 4–5 minutes until thickened and syrupy. Remove from the heat and stir in the crème de cassis. Taste and if too sweet, add a little lemon juice, until the balance of flavours is just right. Strain everything through a sieve over a bowl to separate the berries from the liquid.

Hull the strawberries, cutting the larger ones into quarters and halving the smaller ones, then cover them and chill until ready to use.

With a sharp, serrated knife, slice the croissants horizontally into thirds. Use a rolling pin to briefly flatten each slice then set aside. To assemble the pudding, line the base and sides of a dish roughly 30cm x 25cm and at least 7cm deep with the pieces of croissant. They should overlap slightly but not too much. Be sure to leave enough croissant pieces to create a 'lid' on the top of the pudding. Use a pastry brush to generously coat the croissant lining with some of the berry juice, letting them soak it up thirstily. Spoon some of berries into the dish, then scatter over some of the strawberries, continuing until all the fruits are used up. Pour the remaining juice evenly over the entire pudding, then use the remaining croissant slices to cover it with a 'lid'. Push down on this top layer so that it, too, soaks up plenty of juice. Sit a baking sheet or platter on top of the pudding and put two weights on top – tins of baked beans or heavy bowls will do – to press it all down. Chill overnight. When you're ready to serve, remove the weights and scoop the pudding out into shallow bowls, and serve with plenty of thick cream.

INGREDIENTS

6 day-old croissants
1.1kg mixed berries (roughly
    300g blackcurrants,
    300g redcurrants,
    300g raspberries and
    200g strawberries)
150g caster sugar
100ml water
½ vanilla pod
100ml crème de cassis
1 lemon (juice only)

Serves: 10–12

ICE CREAM SANDWICHES, TWO WAYS

We opened GAIL's Kitchen in winter. If we hadn't already firmly believed that you both can – and indeed should – eat ice cream no matter what the weather, then those first few months confirmed it. That was when the winter version of our ice cream sandwich was born, and it's a dessert that's since developed a bit of an ego, because so many people keep raving about it. The combination of cold ice cream, warm salted caramel sauce and the subtle spice of the cinnamon sugar is what makes it such a hit, and so suited to colder weather. Come summer, we switch to an open-faced sandwich that shows off the season's strawberries in all their brightly-coloured beauty.

WINTER: VANILLA ICE CREAM AND SALTED CARAMEL SANDWICH

This recipe makes more salted caramel than you need – except that we're not sure it's really possible to have more salted caramel than you need. Everyone has to have some salted caramel in their lives, and this will happily keep in the fridge for a week. Begin making the ice cream a day before you want to serve this.

METHOD

Split open the vanilla pod with a sharp knife and scrape out the seeds. Put the seeds and the pod in a saucepan together with the double cream and the milk. Place over a medium heat and bring gently to the boil. In a separate bowl, whisk the egg yolks with the caster sugar until well combined. Slowly pour the boiling cream mixture onto the yolks and sugar, whisking all the time until completely combined, then return the mixture to the saucepan. Stir constantly with a wooden spoon over a low heat until the custard has thickened, but do not let it boil or it will catch on the bottom of the pan and curdle. If it's thick enough, it should coat the back of the wooden spoon and leave a line briefly if a finger is drawn through it.

As soon as the custard is ready, pour it into a clean bowl and sit this bowl inside a larger container full of iced water. Leave to come to room temperature, then chill overnight. The next day, churn in an ice cream machine according to the manufacturer's instructions.

INGREDIENTS

For the vanilla ice cream:
1 vanilla pod
600ml double cream
400ml milk
9 egg yolks
150g caster sugar

For the salted caramel:
100ml water
400g caster sugar
50g golden syrup
100g salted butter, at room
    temperature, diced
100ml double cream
100ml sour cream
a pinch of flaked sea salt

To make the salted caramel, combine the water, caster sugar and golden syrup in a large saucepan. Warm the mixture over a low heat until the sugar has completely dissolved, then increase the heat and bring to the boil. Allow to simmer and cook until you have a very dark caramel. Don't be afraid of the bitterness of burnt sugar, which will add character and depth to the finished dish. Wait until the caramel begins to smoke slightly and is a really dark mahogany, then give it another 10 seconds before adding all the butter and stirring vigorously with a wooden spoon. The mixture will splutter, so stand well back.

Pour in the double cream and sour cream and stir these in well. The mixture will clump as the cool liquids meet the hot caramel, but continue to cook and stir until you have a smooth liquid again. Allow the caramel to bubble for 10–20 seconds more, then take off the heat and decant into a container. Cover and store in the fridge until needed – it will need very gentle reheating in a saucepan to make it liquid again before using.

To prepare the brioche, mix together the cinnamon and the sugar, then dip the brioche slices in it on both sides. Heat a generous knob of butter in a frying pan until foaming, then fry the brioche slices for 3 minutes on each side. They should develop a dark, golden glaze on the outside. You may need to do this in batches and add more butter as you go. Drain on kitchen paper.

Build the sandwiches: each person gets a slice of fried brioche, topped with two scoops of the ice cream, a generous drizzle of salted caramel and a sprinkle of flaked sea salt. Top off the sandwiches with another slice of brioche and push them down with a cake slice or spatula to flatten out ice cream to the shape of the bread. Top with a drizzle more caramel, add another sprinkle of sea salt, and serve immediately.

For the sandwiches:
1 tsp ground cinnamon
100g caster sugar
8 slices of brioche (see p.63),
    1.5 cm thick, 1–2 days old
butter, for frying
flaked sea salt, for sprinkling

Serves: 4

SUMMER: STRAWBERRIES AND CLOTTED CREAM ICE CREAM ON HONEY BUTTER TOAST

Clotted cream is one of Roy's all-time favourite ingredients – it's quite literally the crème de la crème, and you can't go wrong with that. This makes more ice cream than you need for this recipe (unless you're very generous with your servings). Begin making the ice cream a day in advance.

METHOD

Put the milk and half the sugar in a saucepan with a pinch of salt and heat slowly until the sugar has dissolved, then bring gently to the boil. In a separate bowl, whisk the egg yolks with the remaining sugar until well combined. Slowly pour the boiling milk mixture onto the yolks and sugar, whisking all the time until completely combined, then return the mixture to the saucepan. Stir constantly with a wooden spoon over a low heat until the custard has thickened, but do not let it boil or it will catch on the bottom of the pan and curdle. If it's thick enough, it should coat the back of the wooden spoon and leave a line briefly if a finger is drawn through it. When the custard is ready, pour it into a clean bowl and sit this bowl inside a larger container full of iced water. Leave to come to room temperature, then chill overnight. The next day, whisk the clotted cream into the chilled custard and churn in an ice cream machine according to the manufacturer's instructions.

Wash and hull the strawberries, then divide them into two equal portions. Cut one portion into bite-sized pieces and set aside. Blitz the other half in a food processor with the syrup and lemon juice, pulsing only just as much as is necessary in order to liquidise them. Don't over-blitz, or you'll introduce too much air, which will turn the mixture from a deep red to a less striking pink. Pass through a fine sieve then cover and chill.

To make the honey butter, warm the honey gently in a small saucepan until runny, then whisk in the butter a lump at a time. Set aside to cool slightly.

Use a pastry brush to coat each piece of brioche on both sides with the honey butter. Heat a generous knob of butter in a frying pan until it foams, then fry the brioche for 3 minutes on each side until golden and crisp. Build your sandwiches: sit a slice of fried brioche on each plate and top with two scoops of clotted cream ice cream. Toss the chopped strawberries with the chilled strawberry sauce and spoon generously over the ice cream, using up all the berry mixture.

INGREDIENTS

For the ice cream:
250ml milk
150g caster sugar
pinch of flaked sea salt
6 egg yolks
480g clotted cream

For the strawberries:
400g strawberries
90g golden syrup
2 tbsp lemon juice

For the honey butter toast:
40g clear honey
20g butter, at room temperature, plus extra for frying
4 slices of brioche, 2cm thick, 1–2 days old (see p.63)

Serves: 4

RUM BABA, TWO WAYS

Little soft buns, soaked thoroughly in boozy syrup, and served with a dollop of softly whipped cream…this is the GAIL's take on a retro dessert. This is a bit of a cheat baba recipe – we use brioche dough, rather than the classic dough. We already make brioche and use it so often that it seemed only sensible to try it out here, and the result was – we think – even better than the traditional method. We use a special silicon cannelé mould at the bakery. You can find them online, but two mini muffin tins, each with 12 cups, will do the job very well.

Bring the babas to the table swimming in their syrup, in the prettiest serving bowl you own. If you have a cut-glass fruit or punch bowl lurking at the back of a dresser, its time has come. Dust it down and show it off.

SUMMER: PASSION FRUIT AND BERRY

You can buy strained passion fruit purée from specialist shops and online, but if you can't find it, buy a dozen or so passion fruits and scoop out the pulp. You can leave the seeds in, or pass through a sieve if you prefer.

METHOD

Prepare the babas as for winter rum babas (see p.240). To make the syrup, put the vanilla seeds and pod in a large saucepan along with all the other ingredients except the alcohol. Warm gently until the sugar has completely dissolved, then bring to the boil and cook for 5 minutes until you have a light syrup. Remove from the heat and stir in the rum or liqueur. Set aside to cool for 30 minutes, then pour over the babas in a very large serving bowl and leave to soak as outlined on p.240.

When you're ready to serve, prepare the yoghurt cream. Serve three little buns per person, a generous ladle of syrup, a dollop of yoghurt cream, and a scattering of fresh berries to finish.

INGREDIENTS

½ quantity brioche dough
   (see p.63)

For the syrup:
½ vanilla pod, split open,
   seeds scraped out
500g caster sugar
300ml water
100g clear honey
100g passion fruit purée,
   or equivalent passion fruit
   pulp from fresh fruits
1 lemon (juice only)
50ml dark rum or any other kind
   of fruit liqueur you have to
   hand – Gran Marnier,
   Cointreau, Limoncello…

To finish:
yoghurt cream (see p.240)
200g fresh berries, cleaned
   and picked over

Serves: 8

WINTER: SPICED RUM PUNCH

These are even better served with a spoonful or so of Winter Fruit Compôte (see p.101).

METHOD

Butter 24 sections of cannelé moulds or muffin tins if you are using metal ones – there's no need if you're using silicone ones.

First, form the babas: take the cold brioche dough out of the fridge. On a very lightly floured surface, roll it out into a log and slice this into 24 pieces, each weighing roughly 20g. Form the pieces of dough into balls and sit them into the moulds or muffin cups. Cover with a clean, damp tea towel and leave to rest for 1 hour, at room temperature, until doubled in size. They should rise just to the rim of the tins. Preheat the oven to 180°C/gas mark 4. Bake for 8–12 minutes until risen, golden and springy then leave to cool for 5 minutes before turning out. Place all the buns in a large, heatproof bowl.

Prepare the syrup while the buns are rising. Split open the vanilla pod with a sharp knife and scrape out the seeds. Put the pod and the seeds into a large saucepan with all the other ingredients except the rum. Heat gently until the sugar has dissolved, then bring to the boil and cook for 5 minutes to give a light syrup. Remove from the heat and stir in the rum. Cool for at least 30 minutes.

When the syrup has cooled slightly, spoon it over the buns. The brioche is so light and airy that at first the buns will bob on the surface, so use a wooden spoon to dunk them firmly down into the liquid. As they soak up more of the boozy syrup, they'll sink down. Cover the bowl with cling film and leave to soak at room temperature for at least 6 hours, or overnight. Don't chill! To test if the buns are well and truly ready, take one and cut it in half. It should be evenly soaked through all the way to the core.

To make the yoghurt cream, whisk together all the ingredients lightly until it falls in very soft folds. To serve, transfer the buns and syrup to a large bowl. At the table, ladle three buns per person into shallow bowls and top with a generous helping of syrup, then a dollop of the softly whipped cream.

INGREDIENTS

½ quantity brioche dough (see p.63)
flour, for dusting

For the syrup:
1 vanilla pod
500g caster sugar
200ml water
100ml orange juice
100g clear honey
1 orange (zest removed in strips with a vegetable peeler)
3 green cardamom pods, crushed lightly under the blade of a knife to release the flavour
1 cinnamon stick
2 cloves
2 whole star anise
200ml dark rum

For the yoghurt cream:
250ml double cream
50g thick Greek yoghurt
1 tsp caster sugar
1 tsp natural vanilla extract

Serves: 8

BROWN SOURDOUGH ICE CREAM
WITH RASPBERRY RIPPLE

Brown bread ice cream is an old English recipe, and another example of how a genuinely humble ingredient – breadcrumbs – can be elevated to something extraordinary. Here we up the ante by using sourdough breadcrumbs and introducing a ribbon of raspberry ripple.

There's a touch of cinnamon here, too. Raspberries and cinnamon are a match made in heaven – something the French know only too well. It's not a combination you find often in Britain, where we tend to pair cinnamon with more autumnal fruits. But think again: cinnamon and raspberry make the world's most beautiful couple. The warmth of the spice plays beautifully off the tartness of the fruit.

To preserve the almost electric pink of the fresh berries when making the raspberry ripple, it's crucial to avoid over-heating them. The technique we use here leaves their colour brilliantly intact. You'll need to begin this recipe the day before you want to serve it.

METHOD

First, make the caramelised breadcrumbs. Preheat the oven to 180°C/gas mark 4. Blitz the sourdough in a food processor to create fine, but not powdery, crumbs. Empty the breadcrumbs into a mixing bowl.

Melt the butter over a low heat in a small saucepan, taking off the heat as soon as it's liquid – don't let it foam. Stir in the brown sugar, salt, cinnamon and brandy then pour this all over the breadcrumbs and stir well so that all the breadcrumbs are moistened with the butter.

Line a baking sheet with baking paper and spread the buttered crumbs evenly over it. Toast for 25–25 minutes, stirring occasionally so they brown evenly, then remove from the oven – they will dry and crisp as they cool. These are going to be churned into the ice cream, so they need to be really crisp at this stage to hold their crunch later. When ready, set aside to cool.

Make the custard base: heat the milk and double cream in a saucepan over a medium heat until they reach boiling point.

Continued overleaf

INGREDIENTS

For the caramelised
  breadcrumbs:
170g sourdough bread,
    crusts removed (weight
    without crusts)
80g butter
90g soft light brown sugar
pinch of flaked sea salt
1 tsp ground cinnamon
1 tbsp brandy

For the custard base:
200ml milk
300ml double cream
4 egg yolks
80g caster sugar

For the raspberry ripple:
100g raspberries
40g caster sugar

Serves: 4–6

In a separate bowl, whisk the egg yolks with the caster sugar until well combined. Slowly pour the boiling cream mixture onto the yolks and sugar, whisking all the time, then return the mixture to the saucepan. Stir constantly over a low heat until the custard has thickened. Do not let it boil or it will catch on the bottom of the pan or scramble. To test if it's thick enough, coat the back of your wooden spoon with the custard and run your finger through it. If the line you draw stays visible for a second or two, you're there.

As soon as the custard is ready, pour it into a clean bowl and sit this bowl inside a larger container full of iced water. Stir in half the toasted breadcrumb mixture, leave to cool to room temperature, then cover and chill overnight.

To make the raspberry ripple, put the berries and caster sugar in a glass or metal bowl set over a saucepan of water, taking care that the water does not touch the base of the bowl. Place over a medium heat and bring to a constant simmer. The steam will heat the berries and sugar in the bowl above, liquefying the sugar and beginning to sweat the fruit. You should be left with a pink sugar syrup in which the fruit, still intact, will swim. Immediately remove from the heat and blitz very briefly in a food processor to break down the fruit, then strain through a fine sieve to get rid of the pips. Leave to cool to room temperature, then cover and chill overnight.

When you're ready to freeze your ice cream, stir the remaining breadcrumbs into the custard and churn in your ice cream maker according to the manufacturer's instructions. Meanwhile, freeze a large glass or plastic bowl.

Take the well-chilled bowl out of the freezer and spoon the ice cream into it. Drizzle over the raspberry ripple in generous swathes, then take a large spoon and, swiftly and deftly, fold it through using two or three figure-of-eight motions. Do not under any circumstances over-mix or you'll lose the ripple effect – stop before you think you need to. Spoon the ice cream into a lidded container and freeze. This is best eaten within three days of making.

INDEX

Thank you for making this book happen: Emma King, Gerry Moss, Asher Toubkin, Ariana Steigman Bartlomiej Sobanski, Sebastian Fernandez, Monika Malec, Liat Brown, Jonathan Levy, Roz Bado, Joseph Vu, Claire Strickett, Amanda Schiff, James Adams, Annie Hudson, Liz and Max Haarala Hamilton, Charlie Smith, Michelle Noel, Nathan Burton, Lizzy Gray and Laura Herring.
Roy Levy

There are so many special people who have made GAIL's what it is today. Thanks to you all.
A special thanks to my co-founders: Ran Avidan and Gail Mejia for dreaming up GAIL's – and giving us all our daily bread.

For making the bakeries beautiful every day:
Steven Whibley, Ingrid Stabrilova, Martin Barnett, Jagoda Sobaszek, Fabiane De Cesaro, Denisa Nemcokova, Elizabeta Zakolli, Andrea Collingridge, Zuzana Chandler, Fabiana Oppini, Livia Abraham, Pantelitsa Sotiris, Nahouel Kabiri, Cristina Tudorache, Justina Vaznonynte, Krzystof Szczoodruch, Katarzyna Kendzia, Paris Constantinou, Marek Remus and Dusan Urban. Sharon Kazes, Marina De Santos and Aurora Ruiz we miss you!

For sprinkling the magic dust: Romy Miller, Gemma Drake and Anna Goss.

For making beautiful bread and food come rain, hail or shine: Cyril Denecheau, Oded Tomin, Remek Sanetra, Mustapha Rami, Nadesh Karthikess, Nissan Navanesan, Michal Kozlowski, Vlatko Trayonov, Maniwannan Nagaratnam, Ran Amir, Raph Lennon, Dean Arbel, Isabel Kelly, Richard Scott, Catriona Wattsmith, Jake Emerson and all of the rest of the amazing bakery team. George Addison and Richard Fenton I love that you are never too busy to help.

For our amazing teams: Tasbih Imhasly and Desy Rodigari
For juggling the many bags of catering orders: Morgan Cannon
Our oven has broken down saviour: VANESSA!
For our morning wake up coffee: Jessica Worden, Bruno Lombardo and Jelizaveta Vlassova.
Tom Molnar

Thanks to our dear friend and co-founder Emma King,
for working behind the scenes to make this book happen.

14

Ebury Press, an imprint of Ebury Publishing
20 Vauxhall Bridge Road
SW1V 2SA

Ebury Press is part of the Penguin Random House group of companies whose
addresses can be found at global.penguinrandomhouse.com

Text © GAIL's Limited 2014
Photography © Haarala Hamilton 2014

GAIL's Limited have asserted their right to be identified as the author of this
Work in accordance with the Copyright, Designs and Patents Act 1988

First published by Ebury Press in 2014
www.eburypublishing.co.uk

A CIP catalogue record for this book is available from the British Library

Project editor: Laura Herring
Design: Charlie Smith/Nathan Burton
Photography: Haarala Hamilton 2014
Food stylist: Annie Hudson

ISBN 978 0 09 194897 9

Penguin Random House is committed to a sustainable future for our business, our
readers and our planet. This book is made from Forest Stewardship Council®
certified paper

Printed and bound in China by C&C Offset Printing Co., Ltd